Dan Hagedorn

PANAMA CANAL DEFENDERS

Camouflage and Markings of US Sixth Air Force and Antilles Air Command 1941-1945
Volume 1: Single-engined Fighters

Model Centrum PROGRES

Warplane Color Gallery #4

Panama Canal Defenders
Camouflage and Markings of US Sixth Air Force
and Antilles Air Command 1941-1945
Volume 1: Single-engined Fighters

Dan Hagedorn

Published by Model Centrum Progres, Poland
Warsaw, September 2021

ISBN 978-83-60672-34-1

Edited by Wojciech J. Gawrych
Cover layout, design and layout by
PROGRES Publishing House, Warsaw
DTP and prepress by AIRES-GRAF, Warsaw
Printed and bound in European Union by
REGIS Ltd., Napoleona 4, 05-230 Kobyłka,
Poland

First Edition

Exclusive Distributor
Model Centrum
Warsaw, Poland
wjg-books@wp.pl

Dedication
These volumes are dedicated to the memory of
Corporal Robert L. Taylor, 24th Fighter Squadron (SE) and (TE), XXVI Fighter Command,
Sixth Air Force, France Field, Canal Zone, 1943-
1945 and founder of the Air Power Museum,
and to the men and women who served alongside him during W.W.II, each and every one a
member of the Greatest Generation.

Contents

Acknowledgments 3

Introduction 4

Boeing P-26 7

Curtiss P-36 13

Bell P-39 20

Curtiss P-40 46

Color Plates 57

Acknowledgments

These volumes have been a very long time in gestation, and the author is extremely grateful to the publisher, Wojciech J. Gawrych, for recognizing that, at long last, these unsung heroes can be memorialized in this way.

My debt to Dr. Fred Young, Command Historian for what was then the USAF Southern Command at Albrook AFB, CZ between 1965-1969, and my life-long friend and fellow Sixth Air Force historian, the late Robert L. "Bob" Taylor are profound, and it can truthfully be said that none of this would have been possible without the support and tireless encouragement of these splendid Americans.

The numbers of Sixth Air Force veterans who have contributed in so many ways to the realization of this dream over the span of more than 50 years are legion, and it would be impossible to remember them all in these few lines.

I must, however, specifically thank friends and colleagues Dana Bell, Alan Griffith, Jay Miller, David Schwartz, Brian Nicklas, Gerald (Jerry) Casius, Dr. George Cully, Mark Nankivil, Captain Rich Dann, USNR (Ret), Mario Warnaar, Bob Karrer and so many others who resound loudly in my memory.

Last but not least, to the staff of the wonderful Air Power Museum, especially Brent, Ben and Barry Taylor and Mrs. Cindy DeWild for their unforgettable hospitality and friendship, and to son Dan Hagedorn, Jr., who sojourned over many Iowa miles with me in the midst of a global pandemic to locate some of Bob Taylor's treasures and scan them so expertly. And to my sweetheart and lifelong partner, Kathleen, for yet again enduring with love and understanding, yes, "…another project that just has to be done!".

Often cited as "the forgotten air force", the major U.S. Army Air Corps organization charged with overall defense of the vital Panama Canal and all of the Atlantic, Pacific and Caribbean sea approaches, grew out of the between-the-wars organizations known successively as the 19th Wing, Panama Canal Department Air Force (from 19 October 1940) and Caribbean Air Force (from August 1941).

Between 1918 and 1939 – a scant 21 years – the entire Air Corps establishment in what was then known as the Canal Zone operated almost exclusively from two major stations: France Field (later to become known as Old France Field and then when expended nearby, jointly as New France Field or just France Field) on the so-called "Atlantic Side" near the Panamanian city of Colón and Albrook Field on the "Pacific Side", near the Canal Zone administrative center known as Balboa and in the shadow of Panama's major city and capital.

As the world headed inexorably towards yet another World War during the late 1930s, the United States and its amazingly small Army Air Corps – still locked firmly in the grip of isolationist policy as a matter of national direction – commenced the process of, at first, slowly expanding and preparing the defenses of the Canal, on which the weight of a "two ocean" Navy depended.

If the pre-war Air Corps establishment in the vicinity of the Canal was small, that of the U.S. Navy was even more constricted and, although outside the confines of this study, this central set of circumstances led to the historical anomaly which resulted in the USAAC being charged with the aerial defenses of the Canal – including long-range reconnaissance and anti-shipping and anti-submarine warfare. On paper, it was to have rightly been a Navy responsibility but, with the demands of the North Atlantic, Hawaii, the Philippines and the two major U.S. coastal frontiers, the Navy finally had to grudgingly concede that it simply did not have the requisite forces "in being" to dispatch to the region, and thus the Air Corps shouldered the task – a mission for which it was neither trained nor equipped. What few Navy air assets existed in the region were, initially, thus subordinated to the USAAF.

This central set of facts determined all that was to follow, at least for the first two years of the U.S. involvement in what was to become World War Two, and the Navy had not expanded sufficiently toactually assume this responsibility until early 1944.

Like Army Air Corps units in the Continental United States and elsewhere, the Canal Zone based units, which were supported by the small and understaffed Panama Air Depot (PAD), then located at France Field, attempted to expand, train and cope with shortages of every description as the PAD and unit Maintenance Officers argued over often conflicting Air Corps Technical Orders (the legendary "T.O.s")

which seemed to arrive from Washington on a daily basis. While these covered every conceivable aspect of aircraft then in the inventory, they also governed colors and markings, as the Air Corps leadership and the Materiel Division at Wright Field struggled to settle on a "standard" manner of painting its far-flung aircraft inventory. The staff at the PAD often complained that they would receive packages of "new" T.O.s after months of waiting, only to receive a "Priority" Teletype (TWX) message a day later countermanding work that had already commenced.

Thus, for aircraft which were already on hand, Canal Zone-based units, like their brethren in Hawaii and the Philippines, woke up on 7 December 1941, with only a fraction of their tactical aircraft in any sort of "war paint" at all and even these varied widely. The overwhelming majority still wore the colorful, high-visibility pre-war Air Corps array of segmented engine cowling colors, fuselage leadership stripes, and unit insignia. Exacerbating the situation, the various tactical units, crowded onto the two pre-war stations and a new, permanent station under construction on the western side of the Pacific approaches (which was to become Howard Field) almost immediately were dispersed to a dizzying array of remote jungle auxiliary air fields which had been prepared all over the Isthmus of Panama, as the Air Corps leadership at Albrook Field was determined to avoid a repeat of what they were dimly becoming aware had been a disastrous concentration of assets in Hawaii and the Philippines.

It was, therefore, this set of events that was destined to shape the evolution of the manner by which Army Air Corps aircraft in the Caribbean were marked and camouflaged. Stated simply, aside from "factory fresh" aircraft received direct from the United States, such as the major influx of early Bell P-39 Airacobra and Curtiss P-40 variants, and which were, in most instances, already camouflaged by their manufacturers per Specification 24114 of October 1940 (basically, Olive Drab 41 over Neutral Gray), the Caribbean Air Force, which was redesignated as the Sixth Air Force effective February 1942, was on its own – and therein can be found the very basis for this set of books.

There are several specific markings issues which should be set down early in this discussion, however.

First and foremost, there are no known instances within Sixth Air Force wherein "unit codes" were used or painted onto unit aircraft, such as were commonly seen in Europe, North Africa, or elsewhere on USAAF aircraft.

Secondly, Sixth Air Force and Antilles Air Command aircraft operating units relied upon unit insignia (official and otherwise) and individual aircraft numbers for identification, both as so-called "field number" or "line numbers" and for individual aircraft assignments. Many Crew Chiefs, for instance, responsible for painting their pilots choice of "nose art" on an aircraft, could vividly recall the art work and the "field number" (such as "Good old Number 13, Gloria") but made no record of the actual USAAF tail number or serial number whatsoever.

Third, especially during the first six months of the war, aircraft were very frequently moved from one unit to another, in order to maintain at least some semblance of operational readiness. As a direct result, "line numbers" and/or individual "field numbers" quickly became hopelessly intermingled. Typically, the veteran 24th Pursuit Squadron, which had been in Panama since 1919, claimed ownership of "line numbers" between 1 and 15, and units with numbers in sequence beyond 24 assumed the next 15 or so. However, while this worked briefly, the demands of higher headquarters quickly scuttled this discipline, and so these cannot be regarded as reliable indicators of unit assignment.

Likewise, many Crew Chiefs spent the duration of the war in Panama, while their pilots, as quickly as they were promoted to 1st Lieutenant or Captain, were levied for more active combat theaters as replacements. Consequently, there are numerous instances of consecutive aircraft types within a single unit having the same – or nearly the same – nose art applied!

Our examination of the factors which dictated these fundamental realities can be roughly divided into three major chronological periods and, as will become evident in these pages, paralleled the progress of not just the war in the Caribbean but the entire Allied war effort worldwide. Although, as always, there were notable exceptions, these three major epochs may be defined as follows:

About one-third of the entire 16th Pursuit Group P-36A inventory, nine aircraft, are visible in this line-up at Albrook Field, Canal Zone not long after they arrived from the U.S. Only five have unit numbers or unit colors applied, the second aircraft from right being unit number 35 of the 24th Pursuit Squadron. At least two other P-36As are just visible undergoing work – possibly the application of unit markings – in the two hangars in the left background. [USAAC]

Arguably one of the largest and most diverse Fighter Squadrons in the Sixth Air Force, if not the entire USAAF by May 1944, in terms of aircraft on hand, the 30th Fighter Squadron, based at Aguadulce Auxiliary Aerodrome, possessed not fewer than 22 RP-40Cs, two RP-40Bs, 17 P-40Es and a Cessna UC-78, and was essentially a huge OTU. Here we see a line-up of the highly prized UC-78 (camouflaged) and at least 20 assorted P-40s. [Col Delmore E. John]

• 7 December 1941 through December 1943 – Sixth Air Force was obliged, with formal USAAF approval, to evolve its own unique approach to aircraft colors, camouflage and markings, which gradually evolved in no small part because of the extremely long over-water patrols, vast jungles areas, and staggering length of coastal areas and tiny islands which, together, guarded the Pacific approaches – U.S. planners fearing yet another Japanese "Pearl Harbor" strike on strategic Canal installations – and the fearsome demands of the nearly continuous Axis submarine assault in the Caribbean and Antilles region where, indeed, aviation assets were very much in the thick of combat unbeknownst to the overwhelming majority of folks back home. Between February and August 1942, not fewer than 330 surface vessels had been sunk by German and Italian submarines in the Caribbean, its approaches and the Gulf of Mexico alone, and indeed came very close to threatening to severboth the vital crude oil emanating from the Maracaibo Oil Fields in Venezuela and the bauxite for aluminum from the Guianas. The unique demands of these sectors, where squadron-sized units operated more independently than anywhere else in the USAAF establishment, defined the variations in which aircraft were marked. Although there were numbered Commands (such as VI Interceptor Command and VI Bomber Command, and subordinate Group headquarters, these were largely administrative organizations, and individual squadron nominally assigned to each were so widely dispersed as to be all but independent).

• December 1943 through December 1944 – as the Allied victories in the North Atlantic and the Pacific seemed to indicate that a direct assault on the Canal by air and surfaces forces was increasingly less likely, and as the massive U.S. industrial output was finally able to meet both European and Pacific attrition for the most part, the Sixth Air Force was, at long last, able to take stock of its exceptionally wide-spread forces and replenish units which had, in many instances, carried out never-ending operations continuously with the very aircraft that they had been equipped with when the war started. The Command was, at last, able to rationalize its structure, including the creation of the Antilles Air Command effective 20 February 1943, to take over nearly all of the Sixth Air Force assets in the long Antilles chain down through the Guianas. Ironically, this separation precipitated yet another series of brand-new colors and markings deviations, as the AAC attempted to bring order from what the military mind probably regarded at the time as near chaos.

• December 1944 through V-J Day – unbeknownst to the Sixth Air Force and Headquarters, USAAF in Washington, the Japanese had, at the eleventh hour, finally come to the realization of just how fateful and costly their earlier failure to at least make an attempt on the Panama Canal had impacted their entire war effort. Although they never achieved their target, a small fleet of gigantic, aircraft equipped submarines had been commissioned and trained for the specific function of attacking the Canal and its key installations. By this time, Sixth Air Force had, for all intents and purposes, become a gigantic Operational Training Unit and, almost certainly unknown to Japanese planners, had developed tactics and defensive measures which would have almost certainly rendered any such attack a failure in any event. But regulation had finally caught up with Sixth Air Force, at least for the most part, and the previous examples of locally conceived and applied camouflage and markings had all but given way to the "natural metal" regulation seen everywhere. But, even here, Sixth Air Force was granted exemptions, and both its substantial interceptor forces and powerful bombardment elements wore both insignia and underside camouflage seldom seen anywhere else in the USAAF.

Boeing P-26

To the relief of the Army Air Corps pursuit community charged with the defense of the Panama Canal, the first of 26 Boeing P-26As started arriving by air from the Continental United States to, at last, to supplement and eventually relieve the last of the 19th Wing's Boeing P-12 biplanes in late 1938.

Even at that, however, the youngest of the diminutive monoplanes was more than five years old, and all had been flown hard by Air Corps units at Barksdale Field, Louisiana, the last assignment of all but a few, which came from Selfridge Field, Michigan and March Field, California in early 1939. Ironically, the Canal Zone benefitted from the P-26As in that they had been replaced by the new Curtiss P-36A, which would not arrive in Panama in any numbers until August 1939 as the world situation grew ever worse. They were thus, very much, transitional aircraft until such time as more modern equipment became available.

The P-26As arrived still wearing, in most instances, the spectacular pre-war colors, which adorned most tactical types, including squadron insignia and accoutrements.

The Peashooters were issued in small lots to several of the expansion Pursuit Squadrons which were then working up, but none of them were any where near up to statutory strength. The first to receive P-26As were the veteran 24th, 29th and 30th Pursuit Squadrons at Albrook Field, at the time boasting the sole hard-surfaced runway in the Command.

All of the aircraft were initially concentrated at Albrook Field, but gradually they were issued to units which were forming, and most of these spent extended periods at the PCD Training Center at Rio Hato where, finally, the radically understrength operating units finally managed to commence the matter of their colors and markings. The aircraft were worked too hard to budget any time for proper painting at the Panama Air Depot, so Squadron and Group mechanics were left to their own devices, resulting in some very non-standard colors not seen anywhere else.

For most of the young Lieutenants in the Air Corps establishment in Panama at that time, the P-26 was the first monoplane any of them had ever flown and, even though arguably ob-

This is P-26A, with 32P74 barely visible under her port wing – the reverse of what the order should have been! In this case, the yellow wings are retained, but the fuselage has been painted a deep Olive Drab overall, as have the wheel skirts, while the engine cowling is red. Note the hand-crank starting tool in place on the port side of the accessory area. [Jim Dias]

P-26A 65/32P wears the unit number and codes for the 32nd Pursuit Group (I) on her vertical fin, but still has her former 37P65 codes of the 37th Pursuit Group (I) under her port wing, suggesting that unit numbers were repeated – easing the painting duties of the undermanned ground crews. Her fuselage is a very faded Olive Drab, while her vertical fin, wheel covers and an unusual area around the root of the horizontal stabilizer, as well as her engine cowling were white. The tools used to rotate the engine to change her plugs are of interest. The aircraft was not armed at the time of this photo at Rio Hato. [Jim Dias]

P-26A 75/32P was assigned to the 32nd Pursuit Group (I) and floated between the three subordinate squadrons, the 51st, 52nd and 53rd, but was nominally assigned to the latter administratively. The unit returned to France Field from Rio Hato two days after Pearl Harbor. This aircraft has an Olive Drab fuselage, yellow wings and vertical stabilizer, with white engine cowling and wheel covers. [Jim Dias]

Unfortunately, the identity of this 32nd PG (I) P-26A is unknown, but like many of her brethren, she had previously been assigned to the 37th PG (I) and retained the white engine cowling and wheel covers, as well as the semi-gloss Olive Drab fuselage and yellow wings. It is worth noting, however, that in this instance, her radio mast has been painted white as well! She also has the rarely seen A-3 bomb racks in place under her centerline. [Jim Dias]

solescent, most of them were thrilled by the comparatively high performance of the fixed-gear monoplanes. If the P-26 had a single glaring shortcoming, however, it was to be found in their very close-coupled many landing gear and higher landing speeds. These two factors, combined with the notorious shortcoming of France Field (constructed from silt dredged from the construction of the Canal, as was most of Albrook Field), resulted in numerous landing accidents. Even as early as 1939, when the hard-surface main runway at Albrook was finally extended, you could stand at one end and see the undulations in the runway surface in the distance, caused by the silt upon which it was built, slowly settled. As use increased, despite almost constant corrective measures, it only got worse.

Two P-26As were lost to accidents in 1939 – but, ironically, not to landing accidents, as might be expected, but to another aspect of flying around the Canal Zone that was always omnipresent – both as the result of having to ditch at sea in February and July – with the result that, by August, the overall strength had already been reduced to 24 aircraft. Of these, at any one time, only about half were ever combat-ready.

Further accidents followed. During calendar year 1940, due to the intense training regime, not fewer than 17 accidents involving P-26As followed, of which all but two were, miraculously, recovered and returned to service.

By April 1941, the total census of effective P-26As available in the Panama Canal Department (PCD) had dropped to 20, of which eight were assigned in a floating basis to the form-

Through much of 1942 and into 1943, the Panama Interceptor Command Detachment at Guatemala City's La Aurora Field hosted P-26As, including AC33-49 (marked here as 3049), very possibly the solitary USAAF Peashooter to ever be adorned with a form of "nose art". Barely discernible, the aircraft is actually in two-tone upper camouflage, with light gray undersides – although the wheel covers appear to have been a different color. The female figurine is said to have been applied with chalk colors, with a combination of obvious flesh tones, blond hair, and a red bathing suit. [Edward Harrington via Fred Johnsen]

The remains of P-26A 32/37P, probably AC33-32, which went in near Rio Hato on 27 June 1941 while being flown by Lt Herbert K. Anderson. [Jim Dias]

Candidate for the most extraordinary USAAC P-26 color scheme, this aircraft is believed to have been the one retained by Headquarters, 16th Pursuit Group, AC33-125 (by which time it would have appeared on the vertical fin in black as 3125) into early 1943 for the exclusive use of the Group Commander. The "hawk legs" were silver with black detailing, while the "claws" were white, and the "legs" were painted on both the inside as well as the outsides of the wheel pants. The black ball on the fuselage with a white numeral 9 is itself on a white disk, and the inside of the cockpit door, hanging down, and headrest were yellow. [Via David W. Ostrowski]

By the time this image of FAG-48 was taken late in W.W.II, the distinctive "Mayan Warrior" insignia on the fuselage had, for some reason, been overpainted rather crudely with a blue/green paint, while the rest of the fuselage and wings were Olive Drab. While many sources have cited the engine cowling as having been red by this time, it was in fact either gloss black or gloss deep green, with white serials fore and aft. [Via Dr. Gary Kuhn]

ing squadrons of the 32nd and 37th Pursuit Groups. Units known to have operated P-26As included the 28th, 29th, 30th, 31st and 53rd Pursuit Squadrons.

The training strain increased even further, however, and during the course of 1941, 17 more accidents were sustained, many of them fatal to their young pilots and resulting in total losses. By 30 December, just 11 of the original 26 aircraft received in 1938-39 remained, with three of them assigned to the 16th Pursuit Group, and four each to the 32nd and 37th PGs.

With the Japanese attack in the Pacific, the newly formed Panama Interceptor Command (PIC) became consumed with responsibility to not only defend the Canal and its defense installations in the Republic of Panama, but the aerial communications and resupply route down through Central America as well. As a consequence, PIC established Detachments at two key stations in Guatemala which were the northern terminus and departure point for the very long range patrol bombers launching from Guatemala City and San Jose Aerodrome, Guatemala towards the distant Galapagos on their far-ranging patrol arcs. San Jose had been established as an alternate to Guatemala City, as it was soon realized that the take off from high Guatemala City with a full fuel and ordnance load was hazardous in the extreme. The

[This page] Seven USAAF P-26As of the PIC Detachment were overhauled at the PAD in early 1943 and supplied to Guatemala under Lend-Lease with the curious designation "PT-26A". A seventh aircraft ("for spares") and all P-26A parts in the Canal Zone were included. Guatemala painted their aircraft with dark green fuselages, while the engine cowls remained Olive Drab and a unique "Mayan Warrior" insignia. [FAG via Mario Overall]

patrol bombers thus launched with limited fuel loads, flew to San Jose, topped up, and then proceeded on their lonely, one-aircraft patrols. PIC posted a Detachment of three P-26A to San Jose to provide at least a modest aerodrome defense capability while another Detachment, of six, was based at Guatemala City's La Aurora field proper. One P-26A thus remained on activity duty in the Canal Zone itself by February 1942, assigned to the Headquarters Squadron of the 32nd PG at France Field, while one other was always undergoing overhaul at the Panama Air Depot (PAD), which was also located there at the time.

Sixth Air Force thus gained the dubious distinction of being the final USAAF command to operate P-26As in unit strength, if Detachments could be thus described, long after all others in the service had been withdrawn as Class 26 Instructional Airframes or as Operational Trainers.

The Sixth Air Force fighter strength situation had improved sufficiently by 28 February 1943 that Sixth Air Force could finally recall all of the remaining seven aircraft from their distant Detachments to the PAD for a complete overhaul — and ready them for their next adventures, all of them by this time being nearly 10 years old.

The United States was grateful to Guatemala for its unstinting support of the vital patrol stations located there and, when the Guatemalan's organized their Lend-Lease requisition requests in 1942, they requested seven P-26As, aircraft which they had witnessed first-hand in their country for more than a year.

Official U.S. policy at the time dictated that no combat aircraft were to be supplied to any of the Central American republics under the provisions of the Lend-Lease program. However, the Munitions Assignment Board (Air) – perhaps via an amiable deception on the part of the USAAF or intentional subterfuge – approved Guatemalan Lend-Lease Project GT-27 for six "PT-26A" aircraft which, of course, were properly Fairchild primary trainer, if the designation were to stand scrutiny.

In fact, the Sixth Air Force and USAAF had redesignated its surviving seven P-26As as RP-26As (the "R" prefix at this time signifying "Obsolescent" rather than "Reconnaissance") by May 1943 and, on the 11th of that month, all six (plus a seventh "spares airframe, complete") were handed over to the delighted and proud Guatemalans without fanfare at La Aurora Field, freshly overhauled at the PAD. Delivered in USAAF colors and markings of the day, the Guatemalans wasted no time painting on their own insignia and special markings, although the basic Olive Drab upper surfaces were, initially, retained.

Incredibly, two of these aircraft survived further adventures until 1956-57, by which time they were 23 years old, and then were returned to the U.S. – one surviving with the Planes of Fame Museum in Chino, California, and the other at the National Museum of the United States Air Force – both owing their survival to service with the Sixth Air Force and FAG, in turn.

One of the last known images of a Guatemalan P-26A before being retired and sold in 1957-58, this aircraft has been entirely scrubbed to bare metal, but the engine cowling was red. Oddly, the head rest behind the pilot was a deep orange, while the prominent roll-over structure behind the cockpit was, for some reason, painted light blue with a green outline! This may have been the aircraft acquired by the National Museum of the USAF. [FAG via Mario Overall]

Curtiss P-36

As Germany invaded Poland in September 1939, the USAAC leadership set into motion a prearranged plan to reinforce its garrisons overseas, especially those in the vital Panama Canal.

The plan included the flight-delivery of 30 Curtiss P-36A Hawks, most of them levied from established units at Selfridge Field, Michigan – a number that the Air Corps sorely wished was larger but which, given its obligations to concurrently reinforce Hawaii, the West Coast, and equip a new unit for deployment to Alaska, was simply all that could be spared at the time.

Basically, the idea was to re-equip two full squadrons then in-being in the Canal Zone which were still equipped with a rather motley mix of venerable Boeing P-12E and P-12F biplanes, a type which had been in continuous service in the Canal Zone since 1930, and marginally more modern P-26A monoplanes, which had only just arrived in 1938.

Then, after the fall of France to the Nazi onslaught, the hard-pressed Air Corps dispatched one of the last nearly up-to-strength P-36A units left in the Continental United States, the Langley Field, Virginia based 36th Pursuit Group to reinforce a bare-bones patchwork of air bases that were being carved from the string of island that formed the Antilles from the Commonwealth of Puerto Rico south to Trinidad. Most arrived, after surprisingly incident-free flights, at the brand new Ponce Field on Puerto Rico on 18 January 1941. The 36th PG took just 16 P-36As – all that they had, as they had lost several to state-side accidents before deploying – as equipment for its three very understrength Pursuit Squadrons, which operated alongside a few North American BC-1As sent for navigational training and a single Martin B-10BM as a target tug.

Thus, by the dawn of the fateful year 1941, the newly created Caribbean Air Force (CAC, the immediate lineal predecessor of Sixth Air Force), headquartered at Albrook Field in the Canal Zone, at least on paper, found itself with a combined total of three Pursuit Groups, two in Panama and one in the Antilles, every one of which was understrength, to provide the aerial defense for a truly vast area. To make matters worse, the two Groups in Panama were operating a mix of P-26As and P-36As, and were being tasked to not only train pursuit pilots in operating over the trackless jungles, swamps and coastal areas of the isthmus, but to prepare crews for the transition to Bell P-39 and Curtiss P-40 fighters of more modern vintage which were promised and on the horizon.

A 29th Pursuit Squadron (I) aircraft, P-36A 37/16P, sits alongside 61/16P of the sister 43rd PS, the unit insignia of which varies significantly from the approved design. [Jim Dias]

The cowl markings on this 29th Pursuit Squadron (I) P-36A, 34/16P, posing at the Rio Hato Auxiliary Aerodrome, reveal that she had previously been assigned to the 24th PS, but unit ground crew apparently had not yet had time to remove the markings. Note the wheel covers, unique to aircraft of the 29th PS. The "squiggle" on the fuselage is a censors mark. [Jim Dias]

Unlike the 36th PG's deployment to Puerto Rico in early 1941, the flights to Panama from the Continental United States, usually in groups of three, did not go well for the relatively inexperienced pilots. Three of the P-36As, AC38-46, 38-47 and 38-49, having departed Selfridge Field and progressed in their journey as far as Las Mercedes Field in Managua, Nicaragua by 4 September 1939, had taken off late in the day for David, on the far Western fringe of the Republic of Panama, which was the jumping-off point for the last leg to Albrook Field, when they apparently encountered one of the late-afternoon massive tropical fronts which only those who have flown in the region can describe. The trio just disappeared and were totally unaccounted for quite some time.

When the Air Corps leadership in the Canal Zone was finally brought up to speed on the situation, two 44th Reconnaissance Squadron Douglas B-18s, two Northrop A-17s and a Grumman OA-9 were launched to David on the 5th to initiate a search and, aided by 17 P-36As which had already arrived at David and

Unit number 63/16P was assigned to the 43rd Pursuit Squadron (I), 16th Pursuit Group, and this view reveals how the codes were repeated on the inboard port wing, seldom seen. The discoloration on the fuselage just under the cockpit was from greasy mechanics coveralls and what appears to be a scrubbed off insignia on the rear fuselage is a shadow. [Jim Dias]

While being flown by 2/LT Van H. Slayden, P-36A AC38-42, marked with unit number 17 of the 24th Pursuit Squadron, suffered embarrassment when he tried to take off with an empty fuel tank from Albrook Field, Canal Zone, 7 December 1939. Group identifiers had not yet been applied. Note the diamond on the white engine cowl, the individual aircraft number painted small on the natural metal aft section of the cowling, and that the anti-glare panel did not extend over the front edge of the nose. [AAHS]

were awaiting clearance on to the Canal Zone, started scouring the entire area — with scant information on exactly where to search. They were joined by two venerable Thomas-Morse O-19Es of the 7th Reconnaissance Squadron the next day.

In short order, AC38-47, which had been flown by 2/LT James A. Barnett (and which was still wearing its former Unit Number 73 at the time, as were all the other P-36As — they were not re-marked until after arrival at Albrook) on her belly on a beach on the Matapalo Peninsula on the Pacific Coast of Costa Rica. There was no sign of Lieutenant Barnett.

AC38-46, which had been flown by 2/LT George F. Ranney, and AC38-49, flown by Captain Harry A. Jenkins (although, for some reason, the Individual Aircraft Record card listed the pilot as 2/LT George F. Ranney, an obvious corruption of the name of the pilot of AC38-46), were officially reported as "missing".

Then, the crew of a Pan American Douglas DC-3 reported a P-36A about 18 miles (29 km) Northwest of Cape Matapalo, and what they

This aircraft was a Squadron Commander's mount 33/16P, 29th Pursuit Squadron (I) as evidenced by the high-lighted and edged bands on the rear fuselage and the code, in small characters, just visible and painted in this instance as 16P33 just aft of the leading edge under the port wing. [Jim Dias]

Very seldom illustrated, this P-36A, unit number 10/32P, was assigned to a Flight Leader (evidenced by the diagonal deep blue band on the fuselage, edged in white), 52nd Pursuit Squadron, 32nd Pursuit Group. The unit insignia on the fuselage appears to be similar to that of the 65th Pursuit Squadron, as the 52nd PS never acquired an officially sanctioned unit insignia! Note the pristine 44th Reconnaissance Squadron's Douglas B-18 in the background of this 1941 Rio Hato image, taken on the very eve of Pearl Harbor. [Jim Dias]

thought might be her pilot trudging along the beach, walking in the general direction of Madrigal, Costa Rica.

Another search aircraft spotted a third P-36A in the water off the beach from Madrigal. The crew of the intrepid Grumman OA-9 attempted an open-ocean landing near the floating wreckage, and was rewarded by being damaged for the effort, but managed to taxi ashore, where they found the very lucky Lieutenants Barnett and Ranney. Unfortunately, Captain Jenkins nor his aircraft – assumed to have been the one floating – were never found.

Thus, before they had even joined their units, the total number of P-36As which actually joined the CAC had already dropped from 30 to 27. Before their first four full months of service had ended, in December, CAC had lost eight more aircraft to accidents, at least three of them total losses as the pilots of the 24th Pursuit Squadron, which the CAC had planned to fully equip with the "new" P-36s, struggled to acquaint themselves with the retractable gear, high-performance aircraft – a bit more than an easy step-up from P-12s and P-26As.

As the P-36As were assimilated into the CAC, during the first month or two, they retained remnants of the stateside markings they had worn at Selfridge and Barksdale Fields. The Panama Air Depot (then at distant France Field, some 60 air miles from Albrook), as it received damaged aircraft for repair by way of barge or the Pan-

P-36A AC38-60 limped back, somehow, to Albrook Field from a mid-air collision with another P-36A over the Chame Auxiliary Aerodrome on 4 June 1940, and coded 33/16P, was assigned to the 29th Pursuit Squadron (I) at the time. Note that even the tail wheel is painted with the unit colors, believed to have been red and white. [via Ev Cassagneres]

[Far right] A 32nd Pursuit Group aircraft, 11/32P, was probably assigned to the 51st Pursuit Squadron, and 1/LT Brown, assigned as her pilot, poses with his mount in full tropical flight garb. Note the pith helmet atop his seat parachute. [Jim Dias]

ama Railroad, assisted by efficiently removing the remnants of the stateside markings. However, as the CAC fighter establishment expanded rapidly, many of the P-36As were shuffled from squadron to squadron, and the hard-worked ground crews – most of whom were also new to the tropics and being at the very end of the Air Corps logistics chain of the day – rarely had what they needed, even in terms of proper paint colors or, frankly, truly accurate examples of unit insignia that they were being tasked to apply to the aircraft.

By June 1940, the understrength 43rd Pursuit Squadron had been passed some of the P-36As by the 24th PS and, by October, had also been joined by a few shunted over to the 28th PS with the 29th PS having acquired at least two by December.

Starting around July 1940, in view of the deteriorating world situation, the Air Corps finally issued guidance to its growing organizations to apply camouflage to legacy aircraft already in the inventory. Initially, unit identifiers and insignia were unchanged, but as the dark clouds of yet another world conflict loomed, the Air Corps started to direct the removal of any colors or markings which might detract from the value of camouflage.

In the Canal Zone and on Puerto Rico, these instructions arrived in fits and spurts, and the overseas commands were hard-pressed to not only comprehend exactly what was intended, but

This starboard view of 29th PS (I) P-36A 37/16P, shows that the unit number it is not on this side. Likewise, the diamond is on the cowling nose ring on this side, but not on the port side! [Jim Dias]

The 16th Pursuit Group (I) Commander's aircraft, wearing both the Group crest on the mid-fuselage and the individual squadron colors (red, yellow and blue) edged in white on the rear fuselage and in sections on the leading edge of the cowling. This aircraft, has a very high number-within-unit (39/16P) suggesting, together with the distinctive wheel cover markings of the 29th PS (I), that it had previously been assigned to that unit and retained a mix of markings. [Jim Dias]

The exact status of the 10 P-36As flown to Brazil, as well as their pilots and minimal ground crew for converting Brazilian crews, was very much in doubt, and Caribbean Air Force continued to regard them as U.S. property until late 1942, hence the retention of U.S. national insignia and serials. They were only covered by the Lend-Lease Program retrospectively. This was the former AC38-43, which was one of the first to receive Brazilian serials, FAB-03. Note that there are no national markings on the upper wing surfaces whatsoever. The last digit of the USAAC serial, 3, is just barely visible on the rudder. [J. V. Crow]

the actual wherewithal to carry the instructions out. In Panama, for example, it was found that not so much as a single gallon of the approved "Olive Drab" was to be found, and as a result, the PAD attempted to mix its own using interior paints that had been slated for painting latrines! Unit ground crews, to whom these instructions from on high were, at best, confusing, did the best they could to comply and, in the tropical environment in which they labored day-on-day, usually in the open, the results were predictably diverse. This undoubtedly contributed to some bizarre applications on P-36As, in some instances, having the "latrine paint" applied with mops, as there was not enough to go around, and as a result the finished product appeared diluted.

By 26 April 1941, of the 27 P-36As that had made the trek from the CONUS in 1939, only 21 remained on the 16th Pursuit Group's Order of Battle, and this had been reduced once again due to accidents – many of them landing accidents and "landing gear failures" – to just 17 by 11 June.

Meanwhile, the 16 P-36As of the Puerto Rico-based 36th Pursuit Group – not a single one of which ever reached the sky over the Panama Canal (they may as well have been in a different overseas air force) were, from mid-January 1941 on, having their own adventures. At least two of their prized aircraft were reluctantly surrendered to other units in the aircraft-poor Antilles, one going, for some reason, to the 27th Reconnaissance Squadron, while another was

By 7 December 1941, only a few of the Caribbean Air Force's remaining P-36As had been camouflaged, as the prescribed Olive Drab was simply not yet available in Panama. This otherwise anonymous 16th Pursuit Group P-36A may have been one of those painted "Latrine Green", and note that there is no evidence that the gray underside colors were applied, the aircraft apparently having been painted green overall aside from the national insignia. [Jim Dias]

Although Caribbean Air Force and eventually Sixth Air Force assets, the P-36As of the 36th Pursuit Group, which deployed to Ponce Field, Puerto Rico by 18 January 1941, never served a day in Central America, remaining in the Antilles until the survivors were returned to the U.S. in 1943. The 36th PG three squadrons were assigned colors white, red and yellow, and these four, believed to have been 32nd PS aircraft, wore the distinctive "petal" design on their cowlings in red. [Cecil R. Wells via Gerard Casius]

operated by the 24th Air Base Group at Borinquen Field, Puerto Rico, which was expanding rapidly. The Puerto Rican P-36s that survived were probably amongst the last USAAC Hawks to receive "war paint" as, while maintenance facilities in the distant canal Zone were sparse, in the Antilles they were virtually non-existent at this point.

To the relief of one and all, the 16th PG in Panama got word that they were to receive new Curtiss P-40B and P-40C fighters, as well as possibly Bell P-39Ds, and wasted no time in dispatching its 17 remaining, weary P-36As, to the newly formed cadre of the 32nd Pursuit Group. When the P-40s did not arrive as promised, 14 of the P-36As were briefly returned to the 16th PG (less the 43rd PS), leaving the hapless 32nd PG with just two, as well as a smattering of ancient P-26As. Then, to exacerbate matters, CAC received instructions from none other than the Chief of the Air Corps to select the "best" 10 remaining P-36As (as well as two Douglas B-18s), overhaul them, and dispatch them to Fortaleza, Brazil — with experienced pilots and ground crew — to help cement the U.S. commitment to President Getulio Vargas to keep Brazil out of the Axis camp. Suddenly, there were a scant seven P-36As remaining in Sixth Air Force in Panama, with other still flying in the Antilles where, by December 1942, eight were still being operated routinely.

For its part, Sixth Air Force decided that the few remaining P-36As had some point defense value remaining and so dispatched all of them to what became known as the 16th Fighter Group Detachment (the 16th PG had been so redesignated during 1942) at the remote Salinas, Ecuador Air Base (APO 661), one of the two southern most stations of the extremely long Guatemala City – Galapagos Islands – Ta-

lara, Peru (or Salinas, depending on weather) Pacific patrol arc, vital to the early warning system to defend the Canal from Japanese attempts.

Other Sixth Air Force units eventually acquired some of the Hawks although only individually or perhaps two, including HHS, 40th Bomb Group (1942), the 51st, 52nd and 53rd Pursuit Squadrons (1941-1942), the Panama Interceptor Command (PIC) Detachment at San Jose, Guatemala (1942, which also had the last of the P-26As), the 108th Reconaissance Squadron (1943), and HHS, 6th Interceptor Command (1942).

Meanwhile, in the Antilles, the remnants of the P-36As which had been dispatched there in January 1941 were, remarkably, recalled to the CONUS between 23-25 May 1943, where they became fighter trainers in Texas.

The Sixth Air Force did not condemn and scrap its last RP-36A, AC38-37, until 20 June 1944, certainly a candidate for the longest serving of all USAAF P-36 Hawks.

None of the relatively small number of P-36Cs built went to the Caribbean.

In early 1941, after arriving at Ponce Field, Puerto Rico, the 36th Pursuit Group Commander's aircraft, 1/36P (in the foreground), had the standard Group Commander bands added on the rear fuselage, and the Group crest on the fuselage just behind the canopy. The Squadron Commander's aircraft in the background, however, although indistinct, is probably 10/36P and has an unidentified American football style insignia on the mid-fuselage, which bears no resemblance to either the subordinate 22nd, 23rd or 32nd Pursuit Squadron insignia! What is more, the entire cowling appears to be painted white, with the group "petal" design on the leading edge, but with some sort of logo (possibly an Indian head) painted over it! [via Dave Ostrowski]

Although the P-39 series has been routinely ridiculed by aviation historians over the years since the war, the tri-cycle gear fighter turned out to be numerically the most significant type in the wartime Sixth Air Force inventory.

Delivered to Sixth Air Force units in Panama and up and down the Antilles chain as early as June 1941, the command was unique within the W.W.II USAAF in having operated the type in squadron service, without interruption, from that date until October 1945.

At least 447 P-39s, of four major variants, eventually found their way to Sixth Air Force and Antilles Air Command units, comprising 116 P-39Ds (nearly 33% of the first three major production blocks), 69 P-39Ks, 96 P-39Ns and 155 P-39Qs. Other than the Third and Fourth Air Forces in the Continental United States and the Soviet Union, the command thus had the unique distinction of fielding more P-39s in tactical units than any other wartime command. There was not a single day of the period 7 December 1941 through August 1945, that P-39s were not in line service in the Caribbean.

Sixth Air Force operations and intelligence staff officers specifically recommended P-39s for the unique defense requirements of the command and, unlike elsewhere, found the attributes of the design almost perfectly suited to their war plans. These officers concluded, probably with some degree of certainty, that any attack on the Canal or its far-flung defensive perimeter, would not come from high-altitude bombers but, rather, from low-level intruders, who would necessarily have to launch any such attacks on the Canal's vital installations – locks, dams and power sources – from very low altitude, in order to guarantee any chance of success. These were judged to have to originate from one of three sources, in the following order of probability: carrier strike force, surface vessel launched aircraft or land-based in Colombia, Venezuela or Vichy French possessions in the Caribbean.

What the planners did not anticipate with any degree of foresight, however, was the intensive German and Italian submarine offensive in the Caribbean and Gulf of Mexico which was carried out during the course of 1942 and well into 1943. However, once again, when this threat emerged, the scattered P-39 operating units, operating in concert with Douglas B-18 equipped bombardment and reconnaissance units, were found to be nearly the ideal design

Amongst the first P-39N-1s to be delivered to Sixth Air Force was 42-9338 seen here, with unit number 70 in black. Almost certainly a 28th FS aircraft, based at the Chame Auxiliary Aerodrome in the Republic of Panama, she arrived on 18 March 1943 and was lost to an accident there in September 1943. Note that she has two thin, black stripes around her rear fuselage – most unusual for a Sixth AF P-39, and these may have been leadership bands. She is fully armed, as indicated by the flags on her starboard wing guns. [via Bob Karrer, ICC]

The earliest known photo of a Caribbean Air Force P-39D, two sit in readiness alongside a Curtiss P-40C at La Chorrera Auxiliary Aerodrome sometime after July 1941 with the 31st Pursuit Squadron. Although dated 16 April 1942, this is probably when the image was released. The P-39Ds are not remarkable from a colors and markings standpoint, aside from the fact that they have the squadron insignia on their port doors. Note that all three aircraft have auxiliary drop tanks. The P-40C, unit number 17, has a white forward prop spinner. [NARA, OWI, RG208 via Dana Bell]

for anti-submarine warfare. The concentration of firepower which P-39s could bring to bear could make short work of a surfaced submarine, while their augmented range at low altitude made them economical patrol aircraft, which could be deployed singly or in pairs to cover the relatively short distances between the "choke points" of the entire Antilles chain, as well as the in-close approaches to the Atlantic and Pacific approaches to the Canal proper. These aircraft, during the first 12 months of the war, nearly always also totted a 250-pound (114 kg) bomb or 325-pound (148 kg) depth charge, further augmenting their threat to submarines, whether on the surface or submerged in the often crystal-clear aqua waters of the shallower passages.

P-39 operations in the theater, despite their utility and firepower attributes, were not without incident. Especially in Panama, where P-39s operated with regularity, day-in and day-out in every form of tropical heat, deluge, mud and mire, accidents with the tricycle gear fighter were chronic. At least 305 accidents involving P-39s were experienced, often involving the rather fragile nose gear on muddy auxiliary air-

A 29th FS P-39K, 42-4266, wearing unit number 91, arrived in Panama in August 1942 and is parked in front of one of the jungle revetments at Madden Field. The underside flat white camouflage extends unusually high both front and back, and her upper fin cap is painted flat gray. The exhaust erosion is pronounced and she should be wearing national insignia under her port wing, but it is absent. [via Bob Karrer, ICC]

Probably a 53rd PG aircraft, P-39D 41-7016 suffered an accident at the La Chorrera No. 2 Auxiliary Aerodrome on 4 May 1942. The upper fin cap is flat gray which is believed to have been the earliest known use of special markings on Sixth Air Force aircraft, indicating that the aircraft was assigned to the Panama Interceptor Command (PIC). [via Robert F. Dorr]

This P-39D, with unit number 40 painted in black on the forward fuselage, was probably assigned to the 53rd Pursuit Group's 15th Pursuit Squadron when posed on dispersal at Howard Field sometime prior to 18 August 1942. At this point, individual markings and adornments were still in the future. It was clearly during the dry season in Panama! The 53rd returned to CONUS, administratively, in November, but left all of its P-39Ds in Panama. [USAAF 21553AC]

fields with names like La Joya, Chame, Pocri, Aguadulce, La Chorrera, Madden Dam etc. In numerous instances, the same aircraft suffered as many as three incidents during its service life, and laborious aircraft recovery to the tender mercies of the Panama and Puerto Rican Air Depots were weekly events. In some instances, P-39Ns[1] reportedly lost their empennages in high-speed dives – cause for very serious concerns – prompting the gurus at Wright Field to investigate this dangerous potential phenomenon. They finally concluded that severe winds aloft, peculiar to the tropics, were the real cause, and not any inherent defect in the design or construction. In at least five instances, P-39s, usually flying singly on lonely patrols, and seldom in formations of more than three such as were routine in the Mediterranean, Pacific and the Eastern Front, flew off into oblivion in the vast jungle reaches, and have never been found.

For most of the pilots who were assigned to P-39 operating units, their postings came almost immediately after completing flight training and commissioning. They were young,

This P-39K of the 29th Fighter Squadron has had her markings modified the lower side of the port wing was insignia blue, but the propeller spinner is actually faded gray as is the air intake. 42-4247 was later nicknamed "Grumpy". [Author's Collection]

[Below] P-39K 42-4324 of the 24th FS, unit number 15, in dark green with a flat black or dark blue prop spinner. [Air Power Museum]
[Bottom] LT Rufus H. Risk qualified for membership in the "Caterpillar Club" on 6 December 1944 when he bailed out of P-39Q-5 42-20415, unit number 64, of the 30th Fighter Squadron. Note yet another variation on the stenciling used for the unit number. [USAFHRA]

invincible and for the most part issued orders to a "combat tour" in the Caribbean without the slightest real notion of what to expect. One officer, young 2/LT Ed Doran, waxed poetic about his introduction to the "advanced" P-39, recalling that, unlike P-38s and P-47s he flew later in the war, that "…some of our P-39s may have been old rattletraps but you pulled the '39 on like a pair of pants, it was so small".

Units operating the P-39

While most of the P-39 variants supplied during the war to Sixth Air Force and Antilles Air Command were issued to dedicated fighter units, others went in smaller numbers to other tactical units as well. Following is a chronological census of units of these commands known to have operated P-39s at any time.

• 1st Reconnaissance Squadron (Special) – P-39N-1s from June 1943 until April 1944.

• 4th Observation Squadron (M) – another extraordinarily versatile unit, stationed during the entirety of the war at Borinquen Field, Puerto Rico, by 31 December 1943, this small organization could boast six new P-39Qs, which adorned and brightened a ramp that also included four Curtiss O-52s, three Piper L-4As, two each North American O-47Bs and Cessna UC-78s and single examples of the Douglas B-18 and Stinson L-1. This was one of the few Caribbean P-39 units known to have operated its P-39Qs in a natural metal color scheme.

• 13th Pursuit (Fighter) Squadron, 53rd Pursuit Group – P-39Ds at Howard Field, CZ from 2 January until 10 November 1942. During this brief Sixth Air Force reinforcement sojourn, the unit suffered nine P-39D accidents.

This 29th FS P-39K, while appearing to have a "unit" insignia on her port side door, actually wears a detailed individual devil motif. In this case, the unit number 53 was apparently a contraction of her USAAF serial, 42-4253. Note the two-tone upper camouflage patterning. [via Dana Bell]

• 14th Pursuit (Fighter) Squadron, 53rd Pursuit Group – P-39Ds at Howard Field, CZ and Chame Auxiliary Field, Republic of Panama, from 2 January until 10 November 1942. During this brief Sixth Air Force reinforcement assignment, the unit experienced 10 P-39D accidents.

• 15th Pursuit (Fighter) Squadron, 53rd Pursuit Group – P-39Ds at La Chorrera No. 1 and No. 2 Auxiliary Aerodrome from January 2 until November 1942. During this reinforcement assignment, the unit operated an average of 10 P-39Ds and had eight accidents. It moved to Howard Field in the Canal Zone by September 1942.

• 22nd Pursuit (Fighter) Squadron, 36th Pursuit Group – assigned to Losey Field, Puerto Rico on 6 January 1941 with P-36As. Received its first P-39D in June 1941, as well as five P-40Es (which were redeployed to Panama, making it an all-P-39D unit). Moved to Vega Baja, PR on 13 December 1941 after the Japanese attack but sent a Detachment to distant Waller Field, Trinidad which lasted from 6 December 1941 until December 1942. By February 1942, had Detachments at Beane Field, St. Lucia (three P-39Ds), Waller Field (nine P-39Ds), Vega Baja (five P-39Ds) and main body at Arecibo, PR with eight P-39Ds. Some of these Detachments moved about as

Another 29th Fighter Squadron P-39K, unit number 51 (in black), made use of the handy door space on either side for an individual insignia, which appears to be a Granny with a walker wearing a red sweater, and an over-size brown hand-bag. Note the variation in the flat underside camouflage extending down the length of the nose. Sixth Air Force authorized application of gray or light blue "cloud" splotches to the undersides as well, but these have been positively identified mostly on larger aircraft only, engaged in patrol and anti-submarine missions. [via Dana Bell]

Only 210 P-39Ks were built, and Sixth Air Force received at least 72 of them. Here, 42-4252, unit number 11 of the 24th FS, poses with her pilot, LT James R. Willis, at Albrook Field. Note the small pair of dice painted un the lower nose just above the camouflage line. Unusually, and apparently unique to the 24th at the time, the flat black unit number 11 was outlined in flat white, as is the fin cap. [James R. Willis]

the submarine menace intensified, and were attached to bombardment units — where the P-39 pilots were trained as co-pilots on the likes of B-18s. Aircraft of this unit experienced a number of actions against submarines, as noted further on in this account. The unit's personnel were redeployed back to the CONUS on 23 May 1943, but left its surviving aircraft, which by this time comprised only six P-40Cs and two P-39Ds, in the Antilles, where they were reassigned.

• 23rd Pursuit (Fighter) Squadron, 36th Pursuit Group — assigned to Losey Field, PR with P-36As in January 1941 but moved to St. Croix, Virgin Islands in May and received the first of nine P-39Ds in June, although it also had at least one P-40C. The unit returned to Vega Baja, PR in December and, after 7 December, like its sister squadrons, experienced a dizzying series of Detachments, most of which featured P-39Ds or P-40Es. By January 1943, rejoined at Vega Baja, the squadron could count 14 P-39Ds, five P-40Es and four weary P-36As, several of them still on temporary Detachment at Bourne Field. The unit returned to CONUS, minus its aircraft, in May. Like several other Antilles based USAAF units, the 23rd was alerted (and ordnance actual mounted on its aircraft) for possible attacks on the Vichy French at Martinique, in July 1942 and May 1943.

CPT W. L. Reynolds of the 1st Reconnaissance Squadron (Special) poses with his personal insignia, a lightly armed but belligerent Donald Duck, on his P-39N-1. The fact that there is no exhaust erosion aft of the exhaust suggests this photo was taken late January 1943 shortly after arrival. Note the stenciled instruction on the door in flat white giving instructions for removal in an emergency. [USAFHRA]

When the remaining fighter units of Sixth Air Force were all subordinated to the XXVI Fighter Command when it was activated May 1942, they continued to make use of their own unit numbering systems. However, some time in 1944, the Command instituted a marking system for all subordinate units consisting of red, white and blue symbols on their vertical tail surfaces. This P-39Q-20 "Miss Izzy", unit number 28, of the 24th FS, has its Circle M symbol on its vertical tail surfaces – a blue circle with a red M on a white field. Confusingly, the 24th also used a blue triangle bordering a red M on a white field. The unit also had four "color coded" flights: red, yellow, blue and green, and painted their prop spinners accordingly. [USAFHRA]

2/LT Paul W. Neely of the 29th FS was fatally injured on the night of 2/3 July 1943 when he lost control of P-39K 42-4247 on an interception mission over Chepillo Island over the Bay of Panama. His personal emblem, a characterization of "Bugs Bunny", adorned his port door. Note the complete absence of any underwing national insignia, and the rather abrupt demarcation line and two tones of flat white of the nose underside camouflage. [USAFHRA]

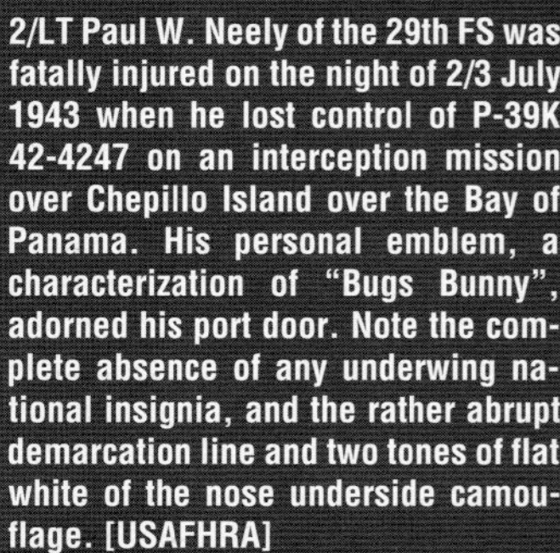

• 24th Fighter Squadron – had been equipped with P-40Cs from the start of hostilities but had received P-39Ds and P-39Ks starting in May 1942, by which time it was stationed at La Joya No. 2, Republic of Panama. By January 1943, it possessed a mix of 17 P-39Ds and P-39Ks but, confusingly, converted over to P-40Ns entirely starting in July 1943. In March 1944, the unit again reequipped, this time with P-39Qs and had 25 on strength by May when it briefly returned to the luxury of Albrook Fields hard-surfaced runway. By 1 February 1945, the transition to P-38s had commenced and, by then back at France Field, where the unit had originated in 1919, it had 20 P-39Qs, two P-38Js, and single examples of the Cessna UC-78, North American AT-6D and Vultee BT-13A.

• 28h Fighter Squadron – had also been a P-40C equipped unit until November 1942 when, stationed at Howard Field, it started the

"Miss Izzy", P-39Q-20 44-3528 again without the crowd in front of her at France Field in 1944. The demarcation between her upper and lower surface camouflage is virtually indistinguishable. [Robert Taylor, Crew Chief]

Unfortunately, the identity of this P-39N-5 "Yankee Doodle", unit number 41, of the veteran 32nd FS, is unknown. Just ahead of the red/white/blue top hat, stenciled diagonally, are the servicing instructions "Remove Tank Before Going into Combat see T.O.81-1-85". This aircraft has carefully applied, pointed blast-tube covers on her port wing guns and the demarcation line of the underside flat white paint is very carefully applied straight. [Erik Erskamp via Mario Warnaar]

P-39N-5 42-18512, unit number 7, of the 1st Reconnaissance Squadron (Special), in company with another unit aircraft with no apparent unit number. The upper aircraft appears to have had a new port-side door installed at some point. All Sixth Air Force P-39s usually operated with belly auxiliary fuel tanks for added range while operating over vast ocean and jungle areas. [Francis N. Lundry via Jerry Casius]

Another photo of P-39N-5 42-18512 of the 1st Reconnaissance Squadron (Special). Although the prop spinner appears to be painted, it was in fact flat slate gray. Her camouflage is clearly defined, however, although for some reason the leading edge of the vertical fin has been painted flat white. The variation in the paint on the leading edges of the wings is also of interest. The port wing guns have a natural metal area scrubbed off, while the starboard gun blast tubes are fully painted. [USAFHRA]

conversion to second-hand P-39Ds and then P-39Ns, although its main body was operating jointly at Chame Auxiliary Aerodrome, Republic of Panama. The first of 26 P-39Qs were assigned in May 1944 and Detachments were sent to Pocri. By April 1945, this unit had also transitioned to P-38s but, as late as June, with 22 P-38Ls nominally assigned (the unit had hangered its aircraft), still had three P-39Qs on the roster.

• 29th Fighter Squadron — another major P-40C operator, this unit also started the transition to P-39Ks in January 1943, stationed at the time at Madden Field. They received their first P-39Q by July. The unit, like all other surviving Sixth Air Force fighter units, was relieved from its earlier 16th Fighter Group assignment in November and subordinated directly to the new XXVI Fighter Command by which time it had a mix of 20 P-39Ns and P-39Qs – and a solitary

Named for the infamous Mona Passage, portal for the majority of Axis submarines to enter the Caribbean in 1942-1944, "Mona II" was a P-39Q of the 32nd FS pictured here while still at Hato Field, Curacao. Her nose art is flesh colored with dark hair on a blue background, which extends under the name. Her pilot was apparently CPT Virgil Roan and the semi-circular paint of the starboard nose gear door may be simply a shadow. Note the pointed cover over her nose 37 mm gun barrel. [Don Baber via Jerry Casius]

P-40C. The unit, minus its aircraft was transferred, on paper, back to CONUS on 8 April 1944.

• 30th Fighter Squadron – this unit started the war as a P-40B and P-40C operator, but started receiving a few P-39Ds by June 1942 when it was based at the La Chorrera Auxiliary Aerodrome, Republic of Panama, still an element of the 37th Fighter Group. It had P-39Ks by October and, by January 1943, had moved to Anton Auxiliary Aerodrome, Republic of Panama. The unit moved to Aguadulce in June, but retained Detachments at Albrook and Corozal and there started work as described in the text as essentially a giant Operational Training Unit. By December, the unit had 11 P-39Qs, 11 P-40Es, two elderly North American BC-1s, and single examples of the Cessna UC-78 and Beech UC-45F! The last P-39s were noted with the unit in June 1945, when five P-39Qs were still on hand.

The blue triangle, white field and red letter H of the 32nd FS of the XXVI Fighter Command, also based at France Field by the time of this photo. Almost certainly P-39Q-20 44-3850 has the unit insignia on her starboard door, unit number 71 and nickname "Mary Jayne IV" in flat white. Like her sister unit at France Field, her four flights were also color coded by their prop spinners – with the same color codes, except that instead of yellow, white was used as here. [via Robert F. Dorr]

[This page] Cited within the 24th Fighter Squadron as "old number 13", P-39Q-5 42-20407 was assigned to Sixth Air Force on 2 August 1943 – a much earlier date than most readers expect for a P-39Q. In the three views she is pictured with the very high underside flat white camouflage on the fuselage sides. Later, she had gained the XXVI Fighter Command "Circle M" symbol and had been re-painted, with her underside camouflage climbing over the top of the fuselage! Robert Taylor, to whom these volumes are dedicated, became crew chief on this aircraft "...when Corporal Ray Capella was AWOL too often!" [Air Power Museum]

• 31st Fighter Squadron – another 37th FG unit which had started the war as a P-40 equipped unit, in October 1942 surviving P-40Cs were joined by P-39Ds although there is evidence that they may have operated a mix as early as July 1941 at La Chorrera Auxiliary Aerodrome. At Howard Field by June 1943, the unit had P-39N-1s and N-5s, but was inactivated in March 1944.

• 32nd Fighter Squadron – one of the most distinguished and longest-serving Sixth Air Force units, the 32nd had been assigned as an element of the 36th PG to Losey Field, PR in January 1941 and was one of the first to receive P-39Ds in June 1941, when eight arrived to supplement 18 P-40Es. The unit, like other Antilles squadrons, was constantly experiencing Detachments and brief moves, and by June 1943 had Detachments at Dakota Field, Losey Field, Hato Field with the main body at Losey and started to augment its weary P-39Ds with P-39Ns and P-39Qs on 27 June at Hato Field. The unit was officially subordinated to the Antilles Air Command on 3 August 1943 and, finally, rejoined Sixth Air Force in March 1944 when it moved to Canal Zone stations.

USAAF P-39s stationed in the Galapagos Islands literally had nowhere to go, and endless patrols over and around the archipelago looking for an enemy who never materialized were hazardous in the extreme, as there weas only one auxiliary landing ground on the rugged islands. This 51st Fighter Squadron P-39Q-5 42-20397 had arrived at Seymour Field by 27 December 1943, and is seen here sporting the relatively new blue outline to the national insignia, a flat-white unit number 13 and the standard yellow serial/radio call numbers on the tail, plus a flat white fin cap. Despite an accident on 10 February 1944, she survived to return to the PAD in the Canal Zone on 30 April 1945 where she was salvaged. [Air Power Museum]

After the 51st Fighter Squadron returned from the Galapagos in June 1944, the unit was stationed at the comparatively luxurious Howard Field near the Pacific approaches to the Canal. Starting in the winter of 1944, the unit was completely reequipped with brand new P-39Q-20s, including 44-3544, unit number 54, seen here, with the "Circle S" symbol on her vertical tail (blue outline, white field, red S) and a candy-striped red and white prop spinner. Note the exhaust erosion on the fuselage, a perennial P-39 maintenance issue. [Air Power Museum]

P-39Q-20 44-3093 was assigned to the 24th Fighter Squadron (SE) in mid-1944. Her fin cap and prop spinner were flat white, while the unit number 18 was flat gray. The nickname, "Gloria", was painted in light yellow on a red cloud on the doors, while the serial/radio call number on the tail was yellow. [Air Power Museum]

Rarely illustrated, this 43rd Fighter Squadron P-39Q-10 had unit number 18 in flat gray above the nickname "Jeanie" in the same paint, assumed to be the same female figure adorning the port door. The wavy delineation on both the fuselage and wing leading edge of this late 1943 photo, taken at the La Joya Auxiliary Aerodrome in Panama, reveals a rather weary young officer pilot in typical tropical flight garb. [Tom "Doc" Hardeman via Nick DeCarlis]

Unit number 11 was 44-3940, the very last P-39Q-20 assigned to Sixth Air Force. She has a flat gray fin cap and prop spinner but no unit of assignment is known. She went to Class C storage at the Panama Air Depot on 29 May 1945, replaced by P-38s, and was scrapped in the Canal Zone shortly after the end of the war. [Air Power Museum]

• 39th Reconnaissance Squadron, Antilles Air Command – this exceptionally cosmopolitan and "jack-of-all-trades" unit acquired at least three P-39N-5s and two P-39Qs by June 1943, which were joined on their flight line by two examples each of the North American O-47A, Curtiss O-52, Stinson L-1, Piper L-4A and an exotic Beech UC-45B. With but 13 officer and 161 enlisted ranks, the unit was seemingly everywhere up-and-down the Antilles chain, but was home-based at Waller Field, Trinidad.

• 43rd Fighter Squadron – unique in having been the only Sixth Air Force fighter unit to be stationed in strength at remote Zandery Field, Dutch Guiana during the war, the 43rd also started the war with mainly P-40Cs. However, by November 1942, they had been returned to Albrook Field in the Canal Zone, but deployed to La Joya No. 2 Auxiliary Aerodrome, where, by that same month, they had commenced being reequipped with P-39Ks although, ironically, they also retained at least one P-36A. They

Another 43rd FS Airacobra, with unit number 20, reveals a stenciled format, and was a P-39Q-10 which reached the Sixth Air Force on 11 August 1943. The very distinct two-tone camouflage in this La Joya Auxiliary Aerodrome image is very pronounced but must have been taken very shortly after arrival, as the exhaust has not yet eroded the paint on te aft fuselage. [Tom "Doc" Hardeman via Nick DeCarlis]

One of the hazards of being assigned and operating from Old France Field was that any engine failure on take-off or overshoot on landing almost invariably resulted in a dunking into the filthy waters near Colon. P-39Q-20 44-3091, unit number 33, 24th FS (SE), was declared a write-off, and pilot 2/LT Louis D. Rassi survived the 14 February 1945 incident. [USAFHRA]

Although assigned to the 29th FS at the time of this accident, 21 January 1944, P-39Q-5 42-19685, with unit number 60 and nicknamed "Erma J", had not yet had either the unit insignia or a personal markings on the large circular area on the starboard door finished by the "extra duty" unit artist. Since she was declared a write-off, it never was. [USAFHRA]

stayed at La Joya through October 1943 when a few P-39Qs and P-40Ns were added to the mix, averaging six P-39s and 12 P-40s at any one time. Sixth Air Force made the decision to standardize them in P-40Ns and this because sole equipment by early 1944 although the unit had gained a single P-39Q by March 1945.

• 51st Fighter Squadron – destined to spend much of the war in the Galapagos, with small base defense Detachments at Salinas, Ecuador and Talara, Peru, it operated P-40Cs until August 1943 when the first P-39Qs were shipped to the archipelego. Returned to La Joya Auxiliary Aerodrome, Republic of Panama on 4 March 1944 by the end of the year, it had 21 P-39Qs and just two remaining P-40Cs. In a bit of a turnabout, these were joined by P-39Ns, upon arrival at La Joya, these had been joined by

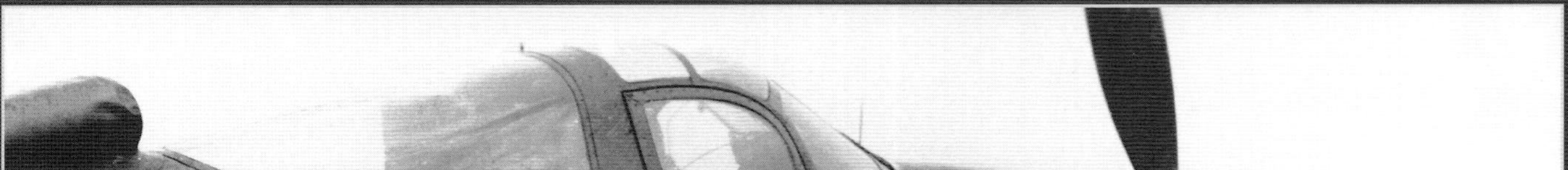

A 24th Fighter Squadron (SE) P-39Q-20 44-3094, unit number 20, sits alert with her pilot's Mae West waiting on the door, adorned with the legacy units insignia. Once again, the vertical fin cap was flat gray in this photo, probably taken at Madden Field. This aircraft survived the war, only to be scrapped in the Canal Zone. [Air Power Museum]

Seldom illustrated, this early P-39Q-5 42-20409, unit number 56, of the 29th Fighter Squadron, crashed on 24 August 1943 at Madden Field while being flown by LT Dion Ellis. Repaired, it returned to service until being lost in a fatal accident on 13 January 1945. The 1943 accident completely ripped off the streamline fairing for the starboard .50 caliber wing gun. Note that the distinctive XXVI FC unit symbols had not yet been added and, as the 29th departed the command administratively on 8 April 1944, it probably was never assigned one for its aircraft. [USAFHRA]

some second-hand P-39N-0s, N-1s and N-5s. The unit transitioned to P-38s starting in November 1944 when it had 23 P-39Qs.

• 52nd Fighter Squadron – yet another unit that had started the war with P-26As, P-36As, P-40Bs and P-40Cs, it started receiving P-39Ds at France Field around August 1942. It was unusual in having a Detachment (E Flight) on the Galapagos by December, although administratively this was redesignated as A and B Flights

The last P-39Q-10 to reach Sixth Air Force, 42-20928, unit number 13, sits alert with two of her sisters with a 20th Troop Carrier Squadron's Douglas C-49 to the rear. Note that the unit number 13 is repeated in black numerals on her drop tank, a fairly common Sixth Air Force practice. The location and unit are uncertain. [via Gerry Asher]

on 1 December. By June 1943, again on paper, the unit was dispersed between Rio Hato and David, Republic of Panama, with a Detachment at Corozal, and its P-39Ds had been joined by P-39N-5s, although it moved to France Field in October. By the end of the year it possessed a mix of 17 P-39Ns and P-39Qs, and a single P-40C. The unit was then disbanded on 25 March 1944.

• 53rd Fighter Squadron – another P-40 operating unit early in the war, the 53rd received its first P-39Ds at Howard Field in April 1943 but operated them only briefly, the unit being administratively returned to CONUS in June, leaving its aircraft and most of its ground crews behind.

Wartime utilization

Below is an examination of the wartime utilization of each of the four production variants which reached Sixth Air Force.

P-39D

The first 43 P-39Ds to reach what was then still the Caribbean Air Force, started reaching units in theater between June and November 1941, as the USAAC accelerated its efforts to reinforce the Eastern Caribbean defense perimeter of the Canal. Virtually brand-new aircraft, these were issued to the Headquarters and Headquarters Squadron (HHS), 36th Pursuit Group at Losey Field, PR (with six, mixed with other types, including P-36As and early P-40s and at least one North American BC-1A) which

[Right and far right] The relative luxury of a concrete hard-standing and runway at Albrook Field on the Pacific side of the Isthmus was a welcome respite for units which had been stationed for extended periods at remote auxiliary aerodrome. This 24th FS (SE) P-39Q-10 42-20924, unit number 44, arrived in the command on 8 September 1943, but did not join the 24th until May 1944. Unusually, she sported a gloss white prop spinner and flat-white, stenciled unit number, plus the "Triangle M" XXVI FC symbol assigned at this point to the 24th. Note that in this instance, her belly tank has been camouflaged and the unit number painted on in stenciled flat white. [Colonel Ole Griffith, USAF (Ret)]

The "Fighting Billy Goat" unit insignia of the 51st Fighter Squadron adorns the starboard door of P-39Q, unit number 92, and sports a flat white fin cap. [via Colby R. Karr]

was stationed at two rapidly expanding bases on Puerto Rico, with detachments deployed to "Destroyers-for-Bases" stations in the Antilles. At that time, the Group had but three subordinate units, the 22nd Pursuit Squadron (which got one P-39D), the 23rd (which got nine) and the 32nd (which initially received eight P-39Ds), although these were quickly augmented as virtually brand-new aircraft were ferried to the Antilles from Buffalo, down the East Coast of the U.S. and, via Cuba, to Puerto Rico. Of the first 112 to go to the Caribbean, 72 were flown to Albrook and Howard Field in the Canal Zone and 40 to Puerto Rico and the Antilles.

At that pre-Pearl Harbor date, these were the only P-39Ds in the Caribbean, and they were not without issues. Shortly after the Japanese attack, the Caribbean Defense Command in Panama got the electrifying message that, of the 43 P-39Ds still on hand (two had already been lost to accidents), only nine were equipped with its principle weapon, the 37 mm cannon. Nine had been deployed much farther south, to Waller Field, Trinidad, to provide aerial defense for the vital oil refineries and shipping in the vicinity and, of these, only two had 37 mm guns. Three others, however, based at Beane Field on St. Lucia, which were specifically charged with keeping an eye on the significant Vichy French naval surface units at Martinique and Guadeloupe (including at least one large submarine and the aircraft carrier "Béarn"), were also fitted with the cannon. Thus, of the aircraft available in the Antilles when the U.S. was thrust

[Above] LT Nutter (left), CPT Troutman (in the cockpit) and LT Rubke admire the newly applied unit insignia of the 30th Fighter Squadron on the starboard door of this P-39Q-20, 44-3089 (note the serial on the lower right corner of the door), 26 February 1945, Aguadulce Aerodrome, Panama. This was one of the largest units in Sixth Air Force, and had 11 P-39Qs, 11 P-40Es, a UC-78, two ancient North American BC-1s and a brand-new UC-45F at the time. The unit transitioned to P-38s by April 1945. [USAFHRA]

[Above right] "Little Devil" adorned the port door of P-39D 41-6931 flown normally by LT Hickey of the 13th Fighter Squadron. This unit returned to the US in June 1943, but left its aircraft in Panama. [Ernest H. McDowell]

into the war, 14 had all of their armament, and 29 did not.

By February 1942, the units of the 36th PG had received a total of 63 P-39Ds, and was nearly up to statutory strength. Still headquartered at Losey Field, PR (where HHS had six and the 23rd PS had 14), the Group was the first to pioneer the distant deployment of semi-autonomous subordinate units. Of these, the 32nd PS at Arecibo, PR was the only squadron that was totally up-to-strength, with 15 P-39Ds, while the 23rd PS, at Losey Field, PR, was close with 14. The 22nd PS, also at Arecibo, had eight P-39Ds there but two Detachments operating at Waller Field, Trinidad (with nine) and Beane Field, St. Lucia (with three). The 23rd PS also had a remote Detachment at Bourne Field, St. Thomas, Virgin Islands.

Meanwhile, the Canal Zone itself had started receiving its first P-39Ds when the units of the 53rd Pursuit Group at the new field (still under construction) on the South Western approaches to Pacific entrance to the Canal, Howard Field had received 13. The HHS, 12th Pursuit Wing, which existed only briefly, and was inactivated on 6 March, also had one.

Nearly all of these "first wave" aircraft wore the simple Olive Drab over Neutral Gray painted on at the factory, and in the hectic first months of the war, hard-pressed ground crews had little time to devote to special adornment, although they soon started at least applying unit insignia to assigned aircraft, almost — without exception — on the P-39s "car doors", either side. The crews quickly realized that these doors made nearly ideal templates for insignia of all kinds, as the doors could be removed and painted during "off-duty" time in the relative comfort of a GP Medium tent or such enclosures as might be at hand, relieving them of the tedious task of

A very well-armed toddler, this was believed to be the individual insignia associated with 2/LT Robert M. Egan, who served with the 51st FS in the Galapagos and, later, suffered two separate accidents flying P-39Qs at France Field. This is believed to be a P-39K, however. The background to the insignia is decidedly a different color than the surrounding Olive Drab. [Air Power Museum]

[Far right] This Amazon adorned the port door of a 29th Fighter Squadron P-39K, the identity of which has eluded identification. [Maury Lauber]

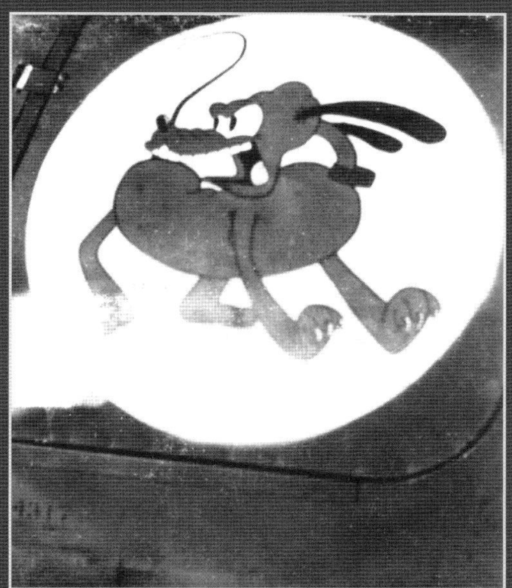

squatting on the inner wing panels in the tropical sun, heat, humidity, and very frequent and torrential rain.

It soon became apparent that some form of individual unit numbers would be a necessity. These designator colors had officially been specified, prewar, to be in yellow, but, in the early months of the war, units "in the field" took it upon themselves to change this to black or, in some instances, black outlined thinly in yellow or white. At the same time, many Groups dropped the pre-war designators (such as 36P, 53P etc.) and retained only the individual number-within-unit on either the vertical fin or forward fuselage – or both.

The myth that the Sixth Air Force and Antilles Air Command were non-combat rear-area commands, perpetuated since the end of the war, could not be farther from the truth, and anti-submarine actions were both intense and numerous. The first recorded P-39D action occurred on 19 May 1942 when two aircraft of the 22nd Pursuit Squadron Detachment at Beane Field, St. Lucia, each dropped a bomb on a surfaced submarine. The first hit, but failed to explode, while the second was about 100 yards off target. On 13 June, two P-39Ds temporarily assigned to the VI Fighter Command Detachment, operating from Waller Field, Trinidad, attacked a surfaced U-boat with their 37 mm cannon and machine guns, but were unable to detect any effect as the sub crash-dived. Then, three days later, on 16 June 1942, two 36th Fighter Group P-39Ds (it had been redesignated from Pursuit that very month), each mounted with a 500-pound (227 kg) bomb, and with all guns blazing, attacked a German submarine – one of at least 12 operating there during the so-called "Merry Month of May," when they were collectively averaging an unsustainable 25,000

[Above left] If a ferocious variation of Disney's Pluto this personal insignia was on both doors of 29th FS P-39K-1 42-4317, which arrived in Panama on 31 July 1942. [Maury Lauber]

[Above] The rather grim visage of "Mickey Finn Esq." adorned the port door of LT S. T. N. Carter's P-39D, 41-6809 – the third P-39D to reach Panama, and was assigned to the 13th Fighter Squadron at the time at Howard Field. [Ernest H. McDowell]

[Below left] This rather liberal interpretation of "Bugs Bunny" also adorned the doors of a 29th FS P-39K. [Maury Lauber]

[Below] Another P-39K of the 29th FS, the pilot was clearly a native of the state of Arkansas – or went to college there, as "Arkansas Traveler" suggests. [Maury Lauber]

This 29th Fighter Squadron P-39K, apparently unit number 40, flown by Captain Webb (kneeling), shows the rather mottled camouflage pattern. [USAFHRA via Dana Bell]

P-39N-5 42-18527 suffered this nose-gear collapse on 6 November 1944 with the 4th TRS. It had a white/red checked prop spinner and the nose art "Pistol Packin' Mama". [Glasebrook Foundation]

tons of Allied shipping a day – 20 miles (37 km) south of Grenada. From available evidence, this was almost certainly U-502. In an action almost identical to that of 19 May, the first aircraft reportedly scored an impressive direct hit on the surfaced sub, which must have surely electrified its crew, but it again failed to explode. The second aircraft missed to one side, but his weapon did in fact explode.

On 1 August 1942, another VI Fighter Command Detachment P-39D flying from Waller Field again attacked a surfaced submarine with guns, but also without visible results. The Airacobras, however, were certainly displaying their worth, and were slowly gaining the attention of the German submarine crews as more than a nuisance.

Two days later, on 3 August, another VI Fighter Command Detachment P-39D again attacked a surfaced submarine. For reasons unknown, however, he could not get his cannon or over-the-nose .50 caliber (12.7 mm) guns to fire and had to resort to just using his four .30 caliber (7.62 mm) wing guns, which required him to get in close. Again, while he saw hits, these were apparently not lethal.

Incredibly, one P-39D survived in the Sixth Air Force Order of Battle as late as 7 October 1944, apparently being used as a training aid at the VI Service Command's training school at Rio Hato Auxiliary Aerodrome, Republic of Panama, although when the Panama Air Depot finally became aware of the existence of the aircraft they immediately declared her excess. Amazingly, and a nod to the overwhelming materiel prowess of the USAAF by that time, 60 surviving Sixth Air Force P-39Ds (of the 116 which had arrived three years earlier) had actually been flight-returned to the CONUS for use as fighter trainers, while two others had been dropped on survey in the Command.

P-39K-1

As the USAAF rushed reinforcements to the Canal Zone following Pearl Harbor, fully expecting a Japanese or even German attempt of some sort on this pivotal installation, factory-fresh P-39Ds were augmented starting in August 1942 by the first of 76 P-39K-1-BEs (of only 210 built of this variant), the last of these being flown by singly and in small groups from San Antonio Air Depot in Texas. These were very similar to the P-39F but had the more powerful (1,325 hp as opposed to 1,150 hp P-39D) Allison V-1710-63 and Aeroproducts props. For historians, the introduction of these aircraft has always posed a dilemma, as other than their USAAF serial numbers, they were virtually indistinguishable from P-39Ds. These were all initially delivered to Albrook Field, CZ which, with Howard, boasted the only hard-surfaced runways in the Canal Zone at the time. Some of these aircraft, joined by some P-39Ds, were the first USAAF fighters to reach the distant and supremely isolated Galapagos Islands by 6 January 1943, and they soon became one of the mainstays of this vital pivot for the extremely long-ranging patrol missions, flown singly from Guatemala City and thence to Salinas, Ecuador or Talara, Peru, by Boeing B-17Es, Consolidated LB-30s, and assorted variants of the B-24. With but one operating field, on Seymour Island, the fighters were the very definition of "point defense" interceptors, and pilots quickly came to realize that any forced landing on the

Every P-39 assigned to Sixth Air Force was received camouflaged — except one. This 51st Fighter Squadron P-39Q, unit number 53 was — for reasons unknown — scrubbed clean except for her anti-glare panel and a red prop spinner, another rarity. LT Bill Schnebel poses with his personal mount. [Air Power Museum]

Another 29th FS P-39K with the personal insignia. [USAFHRA]

87 gallons (383 l) of internal fuel tankage. Difficult to distinguish from earlier P-39Ds and P-39Ks, the P-39Ns retained the seven-gun armament of the earlier variants but standardized on the 37 mm nose cannon. They could also tote a single bomb under the centerline of from 100 to 500 pounds (45 to 227 kg) and were amongst the fastest P-39 variants, being capable of 365 mph (587 km/h) and, at maximum cruise power, a respectable range of 570 miles (917 km) – important in the theater.

The first P-39N-0s arrived in Panama on 18 March 1943, and had been drawn from a batch which had been intended for the British (who in fact planned to pass them immediately to the Russians), accompanied by a number of P-39N-1s as well. Ironically, the first seven of these were not assigned to fighter units but, rather, to the multi-tasked 1st Reconnaissance Squadron, probably much to the delight of the crews, as the other aircraft held by this unit included three North American O-47As and a decidedly elderly Douglas B-18. These were followed by the examples of the definitive P-39N-5 commencing on 19 April. Attrition was heavy, however, and by March 1944, Sixth Air Force could count only 49 P-39Ns remaining in its inventory, down an alarming 47 aircraft in the space of a single year of operation. Of these, 24 were returned to the CONUS in October 1944 while 24 others were surveyed and salvaged in theater and were, significantly, noted by XXVI Fighter Command as "…obsolescent and practically worn out".

Besides the P-39Ns assigned to strictly fighter units of Sixth Air Force and Antilles Air Command, a number of P-39N-5s were also assigned to the 39th Tactical Reconnaissance Squadron in the Antilles as late as September

Compare this image with the earlier view of 24th FS (SE) P-39K number 11 on page 25. Here, the unit insignia is painted on the starboard door, but the underside camouflage demarcation line on the lower nose differs. 2/LT James R. Willis and his crew chief, Sgt. Robert Wilson, at right, give scale to the aircraft. The unit insignia were crafted individually from a master template but differed from one to the next in detail. [Air Power Museum]

extremely rugged islands would not end well. The P-39Ks were notorious, for some reason, in having recurring problems with their main landing gear spindles

A solitary P-39K remained on the Sixth Air Force Order of Battle as late as on 7 October 1944, probably at the VI Service Commands training facility at Rio Hato, while an amazing 49 others had been flight-returned to the CONUS by Ferry Command crews, with five others surveyed and salvaged in the Command.

P-39N-0, P-39N-1, P-39N-5

A major production version, with over 2,000 built, the P-39Ns had powerplant changes once again, the Aeroproducts prop and was somewhat lighter, but at the expense of the loss of

Unfortunately, the serial number of this 36th Pursuit Group P-39D, possibly of the 32nd Pursuit Squadron, named "Pepper", unit number 80, has eluded identification. The camouflage was very mottled, the underside camouflage extended quite far up the nose, and the diagonal stripe was either dark blue or black. Female figures were the exception as adornments on Sixth Air Force fighters, although not so on bombers. The airman admiring the nose art was named Carbonell. [Frank Dutko via Air Power Museum]

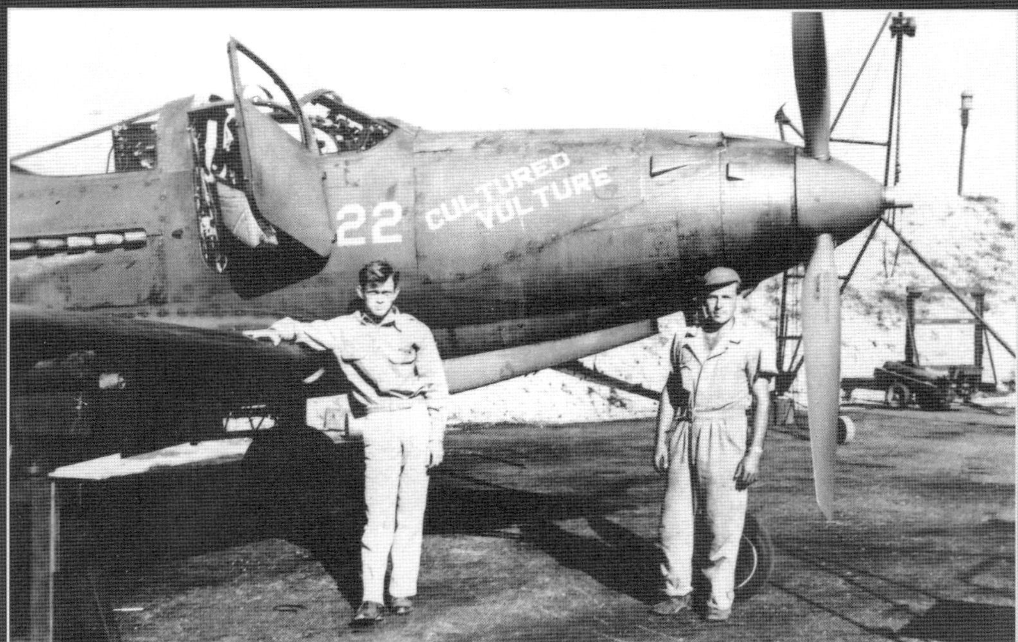

This P-39Q was assigned to the 32nd Fighter Squadron, probably still while an element of the Antilles Air Command at Curacao, and is of interest in that the underside camouflage displays a very even demarcation line, while the upper fuselage of "Cultured Vulture," unit number 22, is extremely weathered, suggesting a very early P-39Q circa July 1943. [Air Power Museum]

1945, and the first four in the Antilles Air Command had been surveyed and salvaged starting in January 1945.

P-39Q-5, P-39Q-20

Hard on the feels of the 96 P-39Ns, the Sixth Air Force started to receive examples of the final production P-39 variants, the P-39Q, on 21 June 1943, far earlier than credited in most accounts, eventually receiving a total of 155. Some of the P-39Ns and P-39Qs went straight to fighter units in the Antilles, notably the veteran 32nd Fighter Squadron.

By March 1944, Sixth Air Force had received 126 of its eventual total of 155, and the Command was set to make the P-39Q its standard variant. A total of 24 earlier P-39Ns had thus been concentrated at the Panama Air Depot by June 1944 and were later (on 10 August 1944) declared excess and salvaged in the Command, along with a solitary P-39D and P-39K, although a number of late P-39N-5s were still in squadron service — as well as a single, long-serving P-39D that month.

The 4th Tactical Reconnaissance Squadron at Waller Field, Trinidad, by that time an element of the Antilles Air Command, was typical, counting amongst its tactical types four P-39Ns and eight P-39Qs. Within Panama and its immediate environs, by October 1944, P-39Qs were posted to active fighters units including the 32nd Fighter Squadron (which had recently been reassigned from the Antilles, where it had been since the early pre-war days) at France Field, CZ (47), 51st Fighter Squadron, Howard Field, CZ (24), 28th Fighter Squadron, Chame

Auxiliary Aerodrome, Republic of Panama (23), 30th Fighter Squadron, Aguadulce, Republic de Panama (12), two were assigned to XXVI Fighter Command's Headquarters and Headquarters Squadron and 27 others were either undergoing work or were in open, Class C storage at the Panama Air Depot.

Not to be forgotten, the 51st Fighter Squadron, which had been stationed on the remote Galapagos Islands for some time, was finally relieved from the isolation and moved to the exquisite comforts of Howard Field, dispatching its mix of 23 P-39Ns and P-39Qs (and a solitary RP-40C!) via surface vessel to the PAD in March 1944 — the last USAAF fighter unit to serve there.

By 27 July 1944, the remaining P-39N-5s and P-39Qs, totaling 108 aircraft, were concentrat-

Probably a P-39K of the 24th FS, this one was named "Glory" for the pilot's wife, and it is worth noting that the rivets around the door frame were either not painted with camouflage paint — or have been replaced entirely. Note also that, as on other 24th FS aircraft, the pilot and crew chief's names are stenciled on the starboard fuselage, just ahead of the door, as well as on the port side as was usually seen during the war. [Air Power Museum]

Unit number 10 was a P-39N-1 assigned to the 1st Reconnaissance Squadron (Special) sometime after June 1943 and, just behind the head of the ground crewman at right, featured what was apparently a personal insignia, an armed "Donald Duck" character. [via Jerry Casius]

ed in the five dedicated, up-to-strength fighter squadrons that were, by this time, directly subordinate to the XXVI Fighter Command[2], which, earlier that year, had adopted tail markings unique to each operating squadron, and which are illustrated in these pages for the first time. The majority of the aircraft were P-39Qs, and they were distributed as follows:

- 24th Fighter Squadron (SE) - 23[3]
- 28th Fighter Squadron (SE) - 24
- 30th Fighter Squadron (SE) - 13
- 32nd Fighter Squadron (SE) - 24
- 51st Fighter Squadron (SE) - 24.

Of these, the 30th Fighter Squadron (Single Engine), perhaps numerically the largest tactical fighter unit in the entire USAAF at the time, was busily engaged at Aguadulce training the Brazilian 1° Grupo de Aviación de Caça (1°GAvC) which eventually deployed to Italy equipped with Republic P-47D Thunderbolts, although at the time they were training, thought was being given to equipping the unit, via Lend-Lease with either P-39Qs or P-40Ns. They completed this little-known tasking on 1 July 1944, and then returned to the full-time status of a line Sixth Air Force fighter unit.

Very rarely illustrated, P-39Q-5 42-20387 arrived in Sixth Air Force on 30 July 1943, but by the time of this 24 January 1945 incident at Howard Field, CZ (APO 832) while being flown by 2/LT Billy M. Tinder, was wearing the "Circle S" of the 51st FS. Note also the candy-cane red and white swirl on the prop spinner. The aircraft was not repaired. [USAFHRA]

As of 12 May 1944, the 30th FS had an astonishing 41 aircraft on strength, the majority of which were a mix of variants of the P-40 but, of these, only 17 were late model P-40Ns. They were slated to re-equip with P-39Qs, which just happened to be the rather well-worn aircraft which had just been returned to the PAD from the Galapagos, and these were exchanged for nine P-39Ns which were also with the squadron.

Final days

By early 1945, Sixth Air Force had received word that, at long last, its entire fighter establishment was to be re-equipped with the twin engine P-38J and P-38L, much to the excitement of the fighter crews, who coveted the additional security of a second engine in flying over the trackless jungles and vast expanses of water. By June 1945, only the 24th and 28th FS (now denoted as "TE" for Twin Engine) still retained P-39Qs, with the former still having five and the latter three, mixed in with their new P-38s.

Of the total of 155 P-39Qs assigned to the Sixth Air Force and Antilles Air Command, 116 survived to be declared surplus in 1945 and, of these, 67 were later salvaged locally.

---

[1] From serial number 42-4944 onwards. Sixth Air Force reported this issue to Wright Field, and the Materiel Command immediately felt that it was caused by the inability of the horizontal stabilizers on this particular series to withstand loads imposed by "severe maneuvers" and immediately imposed the following restrictions, even before full investigation: (1) no abrupt pull-ups followed by abrupt push-overs; (2) no rolls; (3) no other violent maneuvers requiring a reversal of elevator control. Needless to say, these restrictions did not sit well with fighter "jocks" and effectively rendered the sizeable Sixth Air Force P-39N force neutered.

[2] It should be noted that there was also one squadron of the XXVI FC which was equipped solely with P-40Ns at this time, and the HHS, XXVI FC itself had six more. Incredibly, the Command also still had not less than 33 RP-40Cs and three RP-40Bs, which are described later.

[3] As of 1 July 1944, the XXVI Fighter Command had set the T/O authorized strength of each of these units at 25 P-39Qs.

Believed to have been a 53rd Pursuit Group P-39D, the personal insignia on the port door may reflect some relationship to the USC Trojans. Like nearly every Sixth Air Force P-39D, she has two-tone upper camouflage and the antenna blade on her spine appears to be non-standard. [via Ev Cassagneres]

Less than a month after the USAAC leadership commenced deliveries of one of its best front-line fighters, the Bell P-39D Airacobra to bolster the defenses of the Panama Canal and its Caribbean approaches in June 1941, it also directed that its Curtiss-built stablemate, variants of the P-40, also be deployed to the region.

While this same mix was being consummated elsewhere within the enormous expansion program of the Air Corps leading up to the United States entry into the war after 7 December 1941, these two front-line types were destined to be valued and engaged within units of what became the Sixth Air Force in February 1942 quite differently than elsewhere.

As noted in the previous chapter, the P-39 series claimed pride of place as numerically the most significant aircraft in the wartime Sixth Air Force inventory – and this was because of what the type brought to the table in terms of the perceived combat requirements of the Command, especially in terms of its effectiveness as an anti-submarine attacker.

But while this is true, P-40s, perhaps not surprisingly, come in second in terms of sheer numbers, with some 219 of all variants eventually being reflected on the Caribbean Air Force, Sixth Air Force and Antilles Air Command Orders of Battle.

In the beginning, planners at CAF Headquarters in the Canal Zone, charged with organizing and distributing units and their equipment, had little voice in what they were issued by Air Corps Headquarters in Washington. They simply took what was issued, tried to plan accordingly, and, in view of the overwhelming needs and priorities of the far-flung service leading up to Pearl Harbor, were grateful for what they got.

But as the realities of the war that was thrust upon them became more obvious with each passing day, the Caribbean leadership slowly started to provide Washington with an appreciation for what they were facing. Their reports

and urgent teletype intelligence summaries became ever more strident and forceful, especially during the first full year of the war, 1942, when the German submarine onslaught in the Caribbean and the threat of a Japanese invasion fleet appearing over the Pacific horizon seemed not just overwhelming, but imminent. Based on events in the Pacific and the stark reality of sinking ships in the Caribbean approaches to the Canal itself, they struggled to bring their widely scattered units to focal points in the defensive ring.

Thus, while both P-39 and P-40 operating units served alongside elsewhere, in the Caribbean they quickly established what amounted to a symbiotic relationship, many pursuit units being equipped with both types, in small numbers, simultaneously. This unusual arrangement came about because of two dominate factors: firstly, nearly every pursuit unit in the Caribbean was either in the process of forming, often with only a small cadre, and with even fewer aircraft or, secondly, the abrupt arrival of often factory-fresh P-39Ds, P-40Bs and P-40Cs at last enabled the leadership to bring the same

units up to something approaching Table of Organization and Equipment (TO&E) tactical strength – even if it meant taxing the few qualified ground crewmen with as many as four disparate aircraft types to service and maintain.

But the same set of world-wide priorities also conspired to quickly reduce the actual number of P-40s in the theater. Originally, the Air Corps intended to dispatch a nearly equal number of brand-new P-40Cs to both the Canal Zone and to the 36th Pursuit Group, which had arrived at the then-primitive facilities at Borinquen Field, Puerto Rico in January 1941 from Langley Field, Virginia, with an understrength array of Curtiss P-36As.

Instead, between 14 July and 1 August 1941, five used P-40Bs[1] were rushed to Panama, and were initially assigned to the 16th Pursuit Group at Albrook Field. Incredibly, four of the five survived to be returned to the Continental United States (CONUS) between 8 February and 13 July 1944, after seeing very hard use indeed. These five included the very last production P-40B (41-13327). Oddly, however, and not previously reported, two of these (41-5283 and

Although difficult to see in this image, this is 10/16P, probably of the 24th Pursuit Squadron, deployed to one of the mobilization auxiliary aerodromes in Panama, and has two-tone topside camouflage. Her unit number 10 is also worn on the nose just behind the prop, which is painted in two colors, white and what appears to be Olive Drab ahead of the props. [via Gerry M. Asher]

The line-up of a mix of P-40Bs and P-40Cs of the 16th Pursuit Group, probably of the 43rd Pursuit Squadron, shows that this unit used flat white, segmented unit numbers and identifiers, and at this point had two-color prop spinners, yellow and black. They also sported two-color topside camouflage. [via Maury Lauber]

This P-40C, probably 41-13353, presents something of a mystery. The last two digits of her serial are the sole vestiges of her serial. She arrived at Ponce Field, Puerto Rico for the 36th PG on 20 July 1941, but was amongst the P-40Cs ordered returned to Buffalo on 27 October for refurbishment and onward shipment to Russia under Defense Aid, and this may account for her truncated serial. [Dr. Peter Boer via Jerry Casius]

41-13327) were field-modified by the Panama Air Depot (PAD) and formally redesignated as P-40Cs. By the time they were flown back to the States, they had been redesignated as RP-40Cs, as had the two RP-40Bs.

The first P-40Cs built as such arrived at Albrook Field on 21 June 1941, ironically well ahead of the first four P-40Bs, which did not get to Albrook until 14 July. But slightly earlier, on 30 May 1941, the first of 55 P-40Cs started to arrive in Puerto Rico, much to the rejoicing of the men of the 36th PG, which believed they were at long last about to be brought to full authorized strength.

As quickly as they received their new aircraft, the squadrons of the 36th PG started to deploy in Detachments to the several "Destroyers-for-bases" airfields that had been, literally, scrapped out of the small islands up-and-down the Antilles chain, which included Benedict Field on St. Croix, U.S. Virgin Islands, which was at the time important to the U.S. as a primitive, small but strategically located post from whence aerial observation of the Vichy French Fleet-in-Being at Martinique could be surveilled. Unfortunately for young Second Lieutenant Joseph K. Kirkup, it very nearly led

to his undoing and, unwittingly, to his nomination as the first (and only) "ace-in-a-day" in the Caribbean theater, although certainly not under conditions he could celebrate.

Benedict Field was short, soft-surfaced, and literally met the waters edge, and the 22nd Pursuit Squadron Detachment of the 36th PG dispatched there, with at least four of the new P-40Cs, barely a month old, consequently had to be tied down very close to the single runway.

Young Kirkup, upon nearly completing one of his first landings on the island on 23 June 1941, had the brakes on his port (left) main wheel lock up on roll-out, and his P-40C (41-13520), with barely 33.5 hours on the clock, immediately headed straight for four other unit P-40Cs – 41-13515, 41-13516 and 41-13518 – with the result that all but 41-13516 were totally destroyed.

Thus, in a matter of minutes, the effective strength of the 36th PG was effectively reduced even further by four aircraft and necessitated the dispatch of four other unit aircraft to replace them at Benedict Field, once the carnage had been cleared. This debacle apparently did not tarnish his reputation or career, as it was attributed to "materiel failure", and he in fact was

P-40C 41-13362 as she appeared at Ponce Field, Puerto Rico, probably with the 36th PG's 32nd PS in a very worn condition. The units of the 36th PG suffered from very primitive conditions during much of 1941, and this aircraft is unusual in having the last two digits of her serial number 62 repeated in white on her lower nose as her aircraft-in-unit number. Having arrived in Puerto Rico on 16 July 1941 as brand-new, she was transferred, after the U.S. entered the war, to Panama on 12 December and then on to the 16th Pursuit Group Detachment at distant Salinas, Ecuador on the 31st. She suffered an accident there on 23 January 1943, but was returned to the PAD for repair and returned to CONUS as an RP-40C on 27 June 1944. Note that she totes a 250 pound (113 kg) bomb under her centerline. [via Nick Veronico]

elevated to the Command of the 22nd Fighter Squadron by June 1943 – although he never completely lived his experience down.

To this point, all of the P-40Bs and P-40Cs earmarked for dispatch to the Caribbean were marked with the then standard Olive Drab over Light Gray camouflage as applied at the factory, with pre-war U.S. national insignia in two wing positions, the rudder stripes and "U.S. Army" in large black characters under the span of the wings.

Then, suddenly, to the dismay of the 36th PG, urgent orders were received to flight deliver not fewer than 31 of their surviving new P-40Cs, by serial number, back to the Curtiss factory at Buffalo starting around 27 October 1941, where all but a few of them were inspected, repaired as necessary, and then prepared for shipment under the Defense Aid Program (predecessor of Lend-Lease) to the Soviet Union in December. Not surprisingly, the men of the 36th PG, which had only just started working up each of its three squadrons with the aircraft, were perplexed in the extreme, and none of them had any idea that many of the very aircraft they had welcomed only months before would soon be in desperate combat on the Eastern Front.

Thus, in the span of four months, the actual total of P-40s that eventually reached Sixth Air Force units plummeted from the total cited above, 219, to just 188.

The 36th PG was mollified by the news that their P-40Cs were to be replaced by brand-new, six-gun P-40Es, and this is how the three squadrons of the 36th PG operating in the Antilles suddenly found themselves with four different primary mission mounts at the same time, P-36As, P-39Ds, P-40Cs and P-40Es, as will be seen in the brief discussion of P-40 operating units later in this section.

Meanwhile, deliveries of new P-40Cs continued to Panama down through Central America, the last one arriving on 4 August 1941. Shortly thereafter, the first of the 30 new P-40Es, replacements for the P-40Cs they were obliged to ferry back to Buffalo, started arriving in Puerto Rico for the 36th PG, with 17 other making the trip to the Canal Zone starting on 2 October 1941.

Then, immediately following Pearl Harbor, when planners in the Canal Zone suddenly regarded the threat from the Pacific more profound than German submarines, potential commerce raiders, on the Vichy French at Martinique on its eastern frontiers, orders were issued to reassigned not fewer than 17 of the 36th PG's P-40Cs and 18 of its P-40Es to Panama.

Although not as well suited to the task as the cannon-armed P-39Ds, young Lieutenant

P-40 41-13468 was unusual in that, while clearly in the midst of a major P-40C production run, is repeatedly cited on her Individual Aircraft Record Card as a P-40B, suggesting she was retrofitted for some reason by the PAD after arrival in the Canal Zone on 1 July 1941. Here, she is sitting alert in a camouflaged revetment on the West side of Howard Field, wearing the white fin cap of a Panama Interceptor Command (PIC) aircraft and unit number 91 on her nose, with the 31st Fighter Squadron as of December 1942. This aircraft suffered not fewer than five accidents during her service career, the last, on 3 February 1943 in the mountains between Madden Dam and Rio Hato terminal while assigned to the 30th FS. [USAAF 6325]

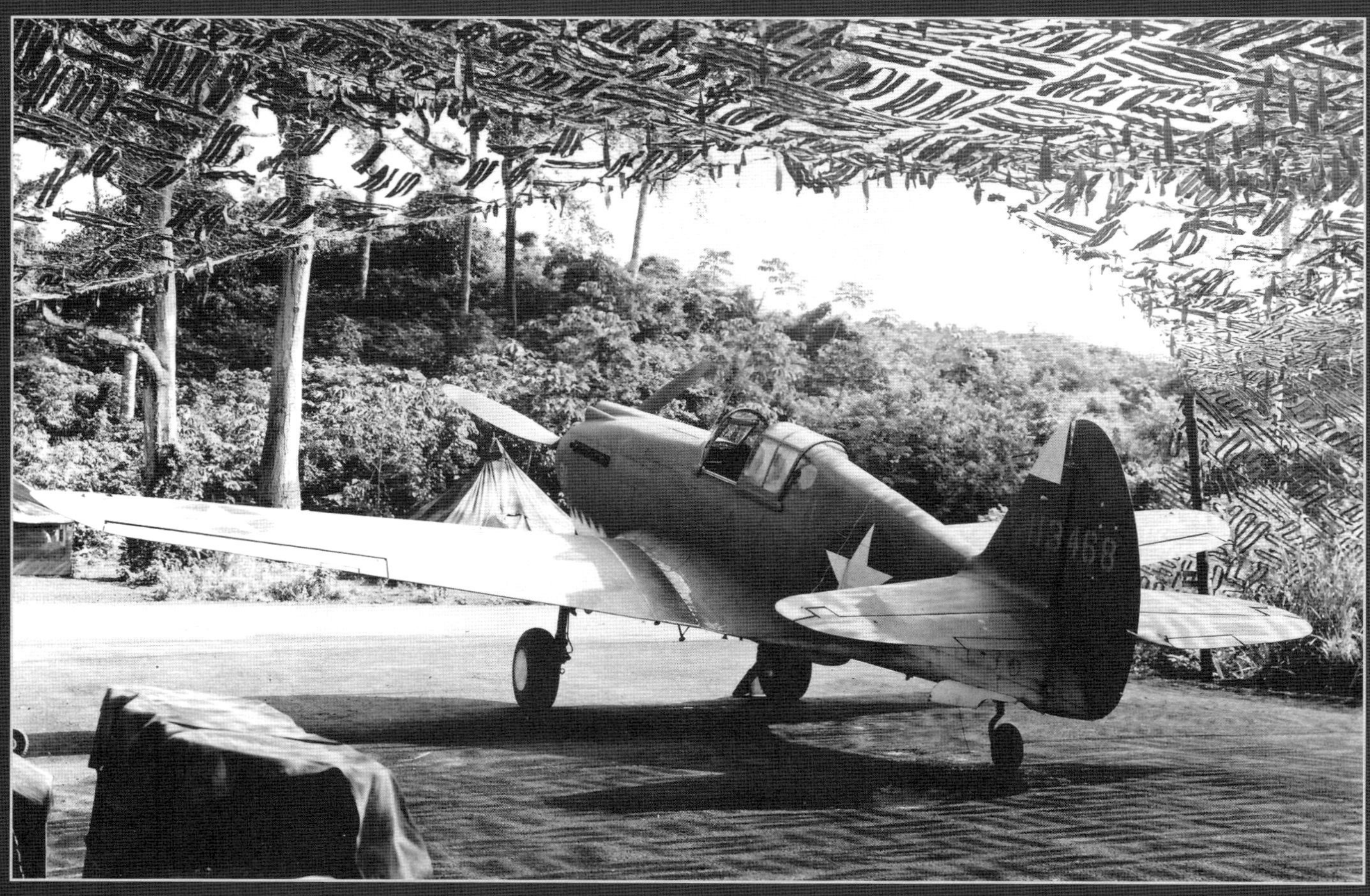

This P-40C, unit number 59, sports special wheel cover paint, applied by her Crew Chief, Sgt. John H. Peck of the 30th Fighter Squadron at the Aguadulce Auxiliary Aerodrome. Probably 41-13359, this is one of the four aircraft which flew into a massive tropical thunderhead near Madden Field, CZ on 7 April 1943 and disappeared. [John H. Peck]

The serial number and operating unit of P-40C, unit number 61, is unknown, but she was amongst the first P-40Cs to reach the Canal Zone and is pictured here, showing her two-tone upper camouflage to good advantage, at the Rio Hato Auxiliary Aerodrome, Panama in late 1941. [Jim Dias]

Gordon Willett recalled that his 16th PG unit, pooling its few P-40Bs and P-40Cs, flew nearly constant anti-submarine patrols over both the Pacific as well as Atlantic/Caribbean approaches to the Canal in the first weeks of the war.

This completed the first, rather spastic P-40 deliveries and within-theater reassignments of what we will term the "first wave" to Caribbean based Air Corps units.

Caribbean Air Force was on high-alert in the weeks and months following Pearl Harbor, and an Air Warning Service (AWS) flash alert at 1755 hrs on 7 January 1942 did nothing to calm nerves.

The Caribbean Defense Command, learning quickly from the Hawaiian disaster, had spotted three initial radar sites at strategic points around the isthmus, and had intensified and prioritized the training of the AWS personnel which ringed the Canal. One of these stations on the far southwestern tip of Panama had detected what it described as an "…unidentified, four engine bomber" near the new Auxiliary Aerodrome at Aguadulce, Panama, and the 16th PG immediately scrambled four P-40Cs to intercept.

Despite an exhaustive search, no target was found. The subsequent inquiry found that no CAF Boeing B-17s, the only four-engined aircraft in the region, had been aloft near that location at the time, and the Navy had not yet assigned any of the Consolidated Coronados to the Caribbean. The only other four-engine aircraft that could possibly have been in the air at the time were the few Boeing 307s of Pan American, which operated into the Balboa Terminal at Albrook Field, but none of these were in the Panama airspace, either.

This left CAF intelligence analysts with but one viable candidate: one of the two Focke-Wulf Fw 200A-0s owned at that juncture by the Brazilian airline Cruzeiro do Sol, the immediate successor to the German-controlled Condor, PP-CBI and PP-CBJ, which had been delivered in 1939. An urgent telegram to the U.S. Air Attaché in Rio, however, squelched this suspicion, as he reported both unserviceable at the airport there for lack of key parts.

This left G-2 at the Quarry Heights bunkers (the so-called "Gibraltar of the Pacific") with only one possible conclusion: that a tender-supported Japanese Navy flying boat had overflown the Isthmus. However, as the Japanese destroyed nearly all of their own records near the end of the war which might have shed light on such an expedition, it appears to have been extremely unlikely. Thus, the matter has never been satisfactorily explained.

Mention must also be made, as a point of clarification, of the fact that Sixth Air Force briefly carried two P-40Ks on its Order of Battle, 42-10090 and 42-10100. These two aircraft were, in fact, enroute to Brazil under the provisions of one of that nation's Lend-Lease requisitions when they suffered accidents enroute. The far-ranging recovery crews of the Panama Air Depot managed to move the two to the PAD, which, by December 1942 when 42-10100 was recovered, started to make the move to their new, huge hangars at Albrook Field, and it was followed by 42-10090 the same month. Both were eventually totally rebuilt and moved on to Brazil by 5 March 1943. It is not believed that they were ever assigned to any Sixth Air Force unit, other than the PAD, although they were "test flown" frequently by Sixth Air Force pilots anxious to see how these compared to the P-40B, P-40C and P-40E versions they were familiar with.

By the end of 1942, Sixth Air Force, which frankly had taken a rather dim view of the substantial numbers of P-39Ds and P-39Ks they were being supplied, owing to what was perceived as a pronounced tendency for the tricycle-geared aircraft to suffer badly on the many rather crude Auxiliary Aerodromes that its fighter units were by then routinely operating from. However, as reports came in describing the effectiveness of the P-39s in keeping German submarines from surfacing, and as its aerodrome system was improved, it soon became apparent that – even though the Command had at one point pleaded with Headquarters to replace all of its P-39s with P-40s – the Airacobras were, indeed, nearly the ideal pursuit type for the conditions they were facing.

The hazards of Sixth Air Force fighter operations are well-illustrated by the events of 7 April 1943. Six 30th FS P-40s, a mix of P-40Cs and P-40Es as was common, conducting a long-range training patrol from their home station at Aguadulce (but officially identified as APO 838, Landing Area No. 2 at Rio Hato) to France Field then, via Madden Field, CZ and home, flying in two elements of three aircraft, entered a cloud bank at about 8,000 feet (2440 m). On emerging, the first element was missing an aircraft, while the second element of three was missing entirely. XXVI FC immediately launched a search but was unable to locate any of the four, missing aircraft, such was the density of the Darien Province jungle canopy. The four were RP-40Cs 41-13468 and 41-13388 and P-40Es 40-579 and 40-632.

Around the same time, the Command hedged its bets, however, by taking the position that some percentage of its overall pursuit strength should comprise late-model P-40s, as these could by then be concentrated in single-type units where a "tail-dragger" could be better adapted to local conditions.

This triggered the creation of a unique arrangement within Sixth Air Force whereby only selected squadrons would be issued with the 30 P-40N-5s and 10 P-40N-20s which started to arrive in Panama on 19 June 1943, the final "wave" of new-built P-40s to reach Sixth Air

A 43rd Pursuit Squadron, 16th Pursuit Group P-40B or P-40C, 44/16P, reveals the Caribbean Air Force/Sixth Air Force early war top-side camouflage scheme, which was applied over the factory finish at the Panama Air Depot when in for inspection. Note the extremely weathered fuselage. Nearly all 16th PG aircraft were exposed to the Panamanian environment day in, day out through their service. [via Maury Lauber]

Sixth Air Force must be included in W.W.II USAAF numbered air forces to have witnessed a version of the famous "sharks mouth" emblem so adaptable to the P-40 series. This aircraft, unit number 99, of the huge 30th Fighter Squadron, with a proud Captain Delmore E. John posing alongside "his" aircraft at Aguadulce in 1944. Note the belly auxiliary fuel tank. [COL Delmore E. John]

Force. The 43rd Fighter Squadron was unique in being the sole unit of Sixth Air Force to be totally equipped with P-40Ns, the only other unit to ever operate any having been HHS, XXVI Fighter Command.

Even with the advent of the P-40Ns, however, by March 1944, the Sixth Air Force still counted not fewer than 33 RP-40Cs, but only 17 P-40Es on its Order of Battle, some of them still actively engaged on the Galapagos and, by May, the HHS of the XXVI Fighter Command itself still had five.

Two RP-40Cs and, remarkably, 16 P-40Es survived until November 1944, when they were, at long last, declared excess and scrapped in-theater, after most of the other survivors had been returned to CONUS in June and July. The 43rd FS thus became the last P-40 operating tactical unit in Sixth Air Force, and soldiered on as late as March 1945, when they still flew 23 of the original 30 P-40Ns received, five others being assigned to HHS XXVI FC or at the PAD. They commenced turning these in to PAD for Class C storage in May, shortly after VE-Day.

Ironically, the remains of one Sixth Air Force P-40C were found in the Galapagos Islands, the nose and engine still intact, as recently as October 2007, near the former fighter strip on North Seymour Island.

Units operating the P-40

The following units are known to have operated variants of the P-40 in the Caribbean and,

where known, details of their markings are described.

- Headquarters and Headquarters Squadron, 12th Pursuit Wing – one P-40C is known to have been assigned for the use of the Wing Commander as of 30 December 1941.
- Headquarters and Headquarters Squadron, XXVI Fighter Command – XXVI Fighter Command was activated in the Canal Zone on 6 March 1942 and had previously been identified as the XXVI Interceptor Command, constituted on 28 February. Had at least one RP-40C and two P-40Ns by May 1944.
- 1st Reconnaissance Squadron (Special) – the lineal successor to the former 1st Observation Squadron, this unusual unit was operating a mix of tired P-40Es, P-39Ns, North American O-47As and Piper L-4As out of Howard Field by 1944, and was subordinated directly to Headquarters, Sixth Air Force.
- 16th Pursuit Group (I) – the units of the 16th PG had a total of 26 P-40Cs assigned as of 30 December 1941. By 28 February, these had been supplemented by 10 P-40Es, less the 43rd PS.

i) 24th Pursuit Squadron – is first known to have operated P-40Cs by 16 December 1941 and had moved with these to the La Joya No. 2 Auxiliary Aerodrome, Panama by 15 March 1942, and still had a few P-36As on strength as well. The main body started re-equipping with P-39Ds and P-39Ks by May 1942, and all of the units P-40Cs were dispatched with Flight C to provide base defense for the aerodrome at Salinas, Ecuador by 30 June 1942. The Squadron had started conversion from P-39Ds and P-39Ks to P-40Ns by July 1943, by which time it had been reconsolidated at Howard Field, CZ. By October, however, with 20 P-40Ns on strength, the unit was maintaining E Flight at Rey Island in the Bay of Panama and another Detachment at Aguadulce Aerodrome, Panama. The unit moved to Madden Field, CZ in March 1944 and, at about the same time, reequipped with 25 new P-39Qs, thus ending its association with P-40s.

ii) 29th Pursuit Squadron – this unit had been partially equipped with P-36As when it received its first P-40C on 16 December 1941. By January 1942, it was one of the first units to receive new P-40Es. It was, like all other Pursuit Squadrons, redesignated as the 29th Fighter Squadron on 15 May 1942 by which time it had moved from the comforts of Albrook Field to Casa Largo Auxiliary Aerodrome, Panama. Starting in September 1942, the unit received P-39Ks and had totally reequipped with Airacobras by December. However, and rather oddly, while possessing 20 P-39Qs by 31 December 1943, the unit also had one P-40N! The unit was relieved from assignment to Sixth Air Force in April 1944.

iii) 43rd Pursuit Squadron – through most of 1941, this unit operated P-36As but when C Flight was moved to Zandery Field, Surinam on 28 January 1942, it took six P-40Cs, leaving six P-36As at the Pacora Auxiliary Aerodrome, Panama. By February, the main body had moved to Waller Field, Trinidad, but left a Detachment at Zandery. The rapid movements of this unit and its various detachments was typical of the hectic period. For instance, the Detachment at Zandery Field had eight P-40Cs between 1 and 15 February 1942 with eight very experienced pilots, while the main body at Pacora, Panama had six P-40Cs and six P-36As with 13 pilots, of whom only three had more than one year of experience, while between 16 and 28 February it had eight P-40Cs at La Joya Auxiliary Aerodrome in Panama with 13 pilots, of whom only three had more than one year's experience as pursuit aviators. During this period, while nominally still assigned to the 16th PG, the squadron was directly subordinated to the Panama Interceptor Command (PIC). The unit started converting to P-39Ks in August 1942. However, in October 1943, the unit started receiving a mix of new P-40Ns and P-39Qs, and was reassigned from the 16th FG to the XXVI Fighter Command. By December, it possessed a mix of six P-39Ks and P-39Qs as well as 12 P-40Ns. XXVI FC then decided to make the 43rd its solitary P-40N operating unit, and the unit said goodbye to P-39s by January 1944, although it also possessed a single RP-40C (41-13372). By December, the Squadron possessed 23 P-40Ns,

A close-up view of the nose of a 43rd FS P-40N, probably unit number 71, revealing the very worn appearance of her camouflage and, in this instance, only the very forward portion of her prop spinner bearing the yellow and black corkscrew marking, very tightly wound in this case. [Air Power Museum]

two Cessna UC-78s, and single examples of the Vultee BT-13A and North American AT-6D. It commenced transition to Lockheed P-38J and P-38L Lightnings in March 1945 and thus holds the honor of having been the last Sixth Air Force unit to operated P-40s as primary equipment.

• 32nd Pursuit Group – while forming, the very under-strength 32nd PG, based at France Field, CZ, had 15 P-40Cs. By 30 December 1941, with the coming of war, the Group possessed a truly cosmopolitan array of aircraft, including 17 P-36As, three P-40Bs, the 15 P-40C mentioned, 11 P-40Es, four venerable P-26As, two North American BC-1s and a solitary Northrop A-17. These were augmented as of 28 February 1942 by an additional P-40B, and the Group also counted 14 P-40Cs, 10 P-40Es and the two BC-1s all at France Field.

i) Headquarters and Headquarters Squadron – apparently retained the P-26As and P-40Bs noted above during early 1942.

This P-40E 40-568, unit number 40, of the 30th FS, had originally been assigned to the 36th PG at Ponce Field in Puerto Rico in September 1941. Here, she is seen following a belly-landing on 9 September 1944 at the La Joya No. 2 Aerodrome, Panama, while being flown by LT James A. Paley. She appears to have a P-40B or P-40C prop and only two wing guns, which had been taped over. [COL Delmore E. John]

ii) 51st Pursuit Squadron (F) – by 18 December 1941, this unit possessed 18 P-40Cs[2], of which five had faulty oxygen equipment, none had bore-sighted guns and six were unserviceable for various reasons. By June 1942, C Flight was detached to the defense of the patrol anchor field at Guatemala City, taking at least one venerable P-26A with them, while the main body at France Field acquired at least two P-40Bs. By December 1942, like many Sixth Air Force fighter units, the Squadron, at least on paper, was widely scattered, although in fact these "transfers" were in reality merely personnel (pilot) replacements, with Flights A and B at BETA with 11 aircraft (the Galapagos Islands, in reality assuming the equipment of E Flight of the 52nd FS), while C Flight (six aircraft) was at Salinas, Ecuador (the former E Flight of the 24th FS), D Flight (eight aircraft) was at Talara, Peru (the former E Flight, 29th FS) and E Flight was at Guatemala City with the last five airworthy P-26As in Sixth Air Force (formerly known simply as the "Fighter Detachment" there). Perhaps mercifully, or perhaps in recognition of the trauma it had been subjected to, the squadron was reequipped with new P-39Qs starting in August 1943 and, by December possessed 21, all at the Galapagos, although it also still retained two RP-40Cs. These were joined by six P-39Ns in April 1944 and the units association with P-40s had ended.

iii) 52nd Pursuit Squadron – based at Rio Hato at the time of Pearl Harbor, this unit was moved to France Field by 18 December and had 12 P-36As and two P-40Bs. At least four P-40Cs had been assigned starting in February 1942 and, while the main body remained at France Field, C Flight had been detached with P-40Cs to the Galapagos on 3 June 1942, the first known fighter element to reach the remote station. This Detachment ended in December, by which time the unit back in Panama had commenced reequipping with P-39Ds. By December 1943, back at France Field, the unit had 17 assorted P-39Ds and P-39N-5s, but also retained a single P-40C. The unit was disbanded on 25 May 1944.

iv) 53rd Pursuit Squadron (F) – this unit had the distinction of being the first Sixth Air Force fighter squadron to be equipped with new P-40Es at its Howard Field station, having been ordered to Panama from Puerto Rico, bringing 10 with them by 18 December 1941. However, of these, only three were combat ready, the other seven being grounded due to seemingly endless problems with their guns. The problems with the guns, first discovered in Puerto Rico, had been so profound that ground crews had actually been instructed to plug the gun holes in the wings, and the virtually brand-new P-40E suffered the indignity of serving "…only as transition aircraft to the Bell P-39D", and the France Field Commanding Officer was so outraged at all of this that he described the 51st and 53rd PSs with one word: "chaotic"! The P-40Es were gradually supplemented with P-40Cs. Starting in January 1943, the unit operated a mix of P-40C, P-40E and P-39D aircraft, but was withdrawn from Sixth Air Force in June 1943 and administratively reassigned to CONUS.

• 36th Pursuit Group

i) 22nd Pursuit Squadron – upon arrival in Puerto Rico, this outfit was equipped with P-39Ds but after the Declaration of War, still home based at Arecibo, PR by February 1942 it possessed eight P-39Ds, three P-36As, eight

This 24th Fighter Squadron P-40N, unit number 13, appears to have a small personal insignia just aft of the number. [Air Power Museum]

P-40Cs and a North American AT-6, with a Detachment of five other P-39Ds at Vega Baja, PR. By December 1942, the unit had been relocated to Waller Field, Trinidad and had 11 P-39Ds (two of which were on Detachment to Hato Field, Curacao) while it also had a Detachment at Zandery Field, Surinam with four P-40Cs. The unit was administratively reassigned to CONUS in May 1943.

ii) 23rd Pursuit Squadron – also initially equipped with P-39Ds, this unit had at least one P-40C by June 1941, based at Benedict Field, St. Croix, VI. By January 1942, it had also been widely dispersed, the main body remaining at Losey Field, PR with 14 P-39Ds and four P-36As, but Detachments were based at Bourne Field, St. Thomas, VI (with eight more P-39Ds and a mix of eight P-40Cs and P-40Es, and three P-36As). This unit continued to operate this eclectic array of aircraft until May 1943, when it was administratively reassigned to CONUS.

iii) 32nd Pursuit Squadron – this unit moved to Puerto Rico in January 1941 and, by June, was operating with a mix of 18 P-40Es and eight P-39Ds. By June 1942, it, too, had Detachments at Bourne Field, St. Thomas, VI, Hato Field, Curacao and Arecibo, PR, but had added at least two P-36As by October. Apparently recalled to Arecibo by December, the unit could count a mix of eight P-40Es (two of which had been Detached to the 36th FG at Losey Field), two P-40Cs, seven P-39Ds and four P-36As. The squadrons association with early P-40 variants appears to have ended around June 1943 when it was reequipped with new P-39Qs and P-39Ns although a few P-39Ds lingered on. The unit was reassigned from Antilles Air Command to Panama in March 1944 and assigned to the XXVI FC.

• 37th Pursuit Group – activated on 1 February 1940 in the Canal Zone, this expansion unit consisted of the HHS and the subordinate 28th, 30th and 31st Pursuit Squadrons, and by 30 December 1941 they shared 26 P-40Cs, six P-40Es, two P-40Bs, four P-26As and a North American BC-1 between them. Initially stationed at Albrook, the Group moved to Howard Field on 1 September 1943 but was disbanded on 1 November, and its equipment and personnel were absorbed by other Sixth Air Force units.

i) Headquarters and Headquarters Squadron – had four P-40Cs and a single P-40E as of February 1942.

ii) 28th Pursuit Squadron – at the outbreak of war, this squadron was deployed to the Paitilla Point airport, Panama (the former National Airport on the eastern outskirts, at the time, of Panama City) with seven P-40Cs and three P-40Es. Paitilla was not kind to the 28th, at least seven accidents there between February and July 1942 involving P-40Cs. The unit was reassigned to the Chame Auxiliary Aerodrome, Panama in November 1942, but left a detachment of at least three P-40Es at Paitilla Point as late as February 1943, and started reequipping with P-39Ns around May 1943. However, by December 1943, while possessing 19 P-39Ns, it also had a single RP-40C. This was its last known association with P-40s.

iii) 30th Pursuit Squadron – initially being issued a few P-26As in 1940, by 31 January 1942 based at the La Chorrera Auxiliary Aerodrome, Panama, the 30th had eight P-40Cs and a solitary P-40E. It commenced reequipping with P-39Ds and P-39Ks in June 1942. However, apparently this was countermanded and, by May 1943 the unit had been designated as, essentially, a huge Operational Training Unit and

Although Headquarters and Headquarters Squadron, XXVI Fighter Command is known to have had a number of RP-40Cs and P-40Ns assigned, this is the only known photo of one. P-40N-5 42-105299 was assigned on 4 July 1943. A former unit number on her nose had been overpainted with a different shade of camouflage paint, and her XXVI FC diamond emblem on her vertical tail comprises a blue outline, yellow field, and "lazy" letter S. [COL Ole Griffith]

the majority of surviving RP-40B, RP-40C and P-40E aircraft still within Sixth Air Force were assigned to the unit at the Aguadulce Auxiliary Aerodrome, Panama. By May 1944, the unit possessed not fewer than two RP-40B (of three still in the Sixth Air Force), 22 RP-40Cs (of 33) and 17 P-40E aircraft, all that remained of this variant in the Command. By July, these had been joined by six P-39Qs and, by December, the last of the RP-40Bs and RP-40Cs had been withdrawn and unit strength stood at 11 P-39Qs, 11 P-40Es, two ancient North American BC-1s, and single examples of the Beech UC-45F and Cessna UC-78. The last of the P-40Es were surplused to the PAD on 19 February 1945.

iv) 31st Pursuit Squadron – equipped initially with Boeing P-26As, the 31st received its first P-40Cs in July 1941 and converted to brand new P-40Es in November. Following Pearl Harbor, the unit was moved at La Chorrera Auxiliary Aerodrome on 9 December. By 15 February, they had surrendered all but one of their prized P-40Es to other units but had gained seven P-40Cs as replacements and had 10 pilots, of whom six had more than a year of experience as fighter pilots. Reequipment with P-39Ds commenced in October 1942. However, like other Sixth Air Force fighter units, by December 1943, along with a mix of 18 P-39Ds and P-39N-1s, the squadron also had a single P-40. The unit was inactivated on 25 May 1944.

• 99th Bomb Squadron ("Force A") – sent on an urgent basis from the Rio Hato Auxiliary Aerodrome to the newly established Zandery Field, Surinam on 3 December 1941, this unit took eight attached P-40Cs (known at least informally as the 16th Pursuit Group (I) Detachment by January 1942) with it to provide aerodrome security for its small force of six Douglas B-18As, and they had set up shop by 30 December. These were reassigned to the 22nd Pursuit Squadron when it arrived, however.

Afterword

Although they remain untraced, an intriguing entry in the Sixth Air Force chronological diary for 27 March 1944 reported that the Command had received information that four "…dual-seat, dual control P-40s will be delivered in April for the use of the Brazilian training program" which was, in fact, being conducted at Aguadulce, Panama by the aforementioned 30th FS.

Finally, the story of the P-40 in Sixth Air Force cannot be regarded as complete without mention of an engineering report dated 13 July 1943, which speaks for itself and which is quoted in its entirety as follows: "Sixth Air Force G-4, Engineering, is making some 150 dummy P-40 airplanes. These are for issue to the Panama Interceptor Command. We will deliver these as soon as possible and get them out of our way".

---

[1] Oddly, the official Order of Battle for Caribbean Air Force actually reflected a total of six P-40Bs, divided between the 16th (three) and 37th (three) Pursuit Groups by early July 1941.

[2] P-40Cs known assigned to the 51st PS included 41-13359, 41-13360, 41-13361, 41-13362, 41-13363, 41-13372, 41-13376, 41-13388, 41-13509, 41-13511, 41-13512, 41-13512, 41-13516, 41-13519, and 41-13457 (which passed to the 53rd PS).

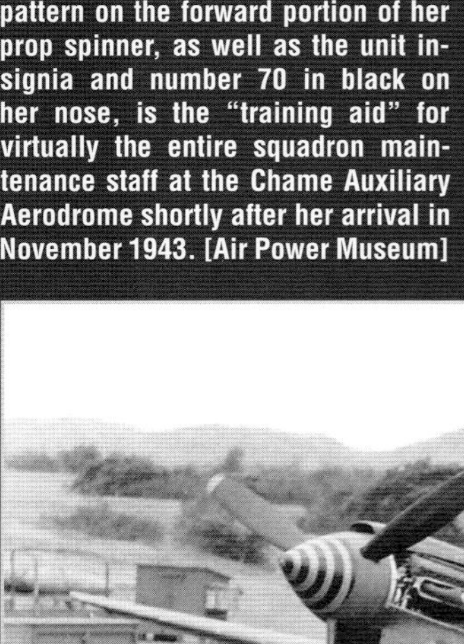

This view of a P-40N-20, probably 43-22892, assigned to the 43rd Fighter Squadron, and bearing their unique "corkscrew" yellow and black pattern on the forward portion of her prop spinner, as well as the unit insignia and number 70 in black on her nose, is the "training aid" for virtually the entire squadron maintenance staff at the Chame Auxiliary Aerodrome shortly after her arrival in November 1943. [Air Power Museum]

Color Plates

Bell P-39K-1-BE Airacobra, 42-4266, unit number 91, 29th Fighter Squadron, Madden Field, Panama, after August 1942. When initially delivered to the USAAF, the aircraft had been standard Olive Drab over Neutral Gray. However, like nearly every tactical aircraft assigned to Sixth Air Force, upon arrival in the Command it was cycled through the Panama Air Depot (PAD) and repainted in theater-specific camouflage. The colors used were apparently Lend-Lease shades of Dark Green and Dark Earth over flat white, the patterns of which varied from one aircraft to the next, with unit number 91 in flat black. Although the fin cap at the leading edge of the vertical fin appears Dark Earth, it was actually flat gray. This aircraft should have had a U.S. national insignia under the port wing, but did not. It had a short service life. It was lost on 4 December 1942, one mile north of the Auxiliary Aerodrome at La Joya No. 2 (some sources cite No. 1) by which time she had been reassigned to the 43rd Fighter Squadron, with fatal consequences to 2/LT Walter R. Howard when he failed to recover from a spin.

Bell P-39K-1-BE Airacobra 42-4247 – the fourth one built – unit number 24, was amongst the first P-39K-1s to arrive in Panama under Project 390, code named "Grumpy", 15–16 July 1942. Assigned to the 29th Fighter Squadron, an unknown earlier unit number had been crudely overpainted and changed to 24 white. The prop spinner was the flat gray color just as it came out of the crate, but the leading edge of the vertical fin tip had been painted flat white, indicating its assignment to a unit of the Panama Interceptor Command (PIC). Once again, there is no national insignia under the port wing and the port wing tip appears to have been a replacement painted Dark Green both top and bottom. The entire air intake assembly aft of the canopy on the spine was also "right out of the crate" in primer. This aircraft later gained a "Bugs Bunny" motif on her port fuselage door, which was worn while flown by 2/LT Paul W. Neely when the aircraft was lost on a night interception mission over Chepillo Island on 2/3 July 1943.

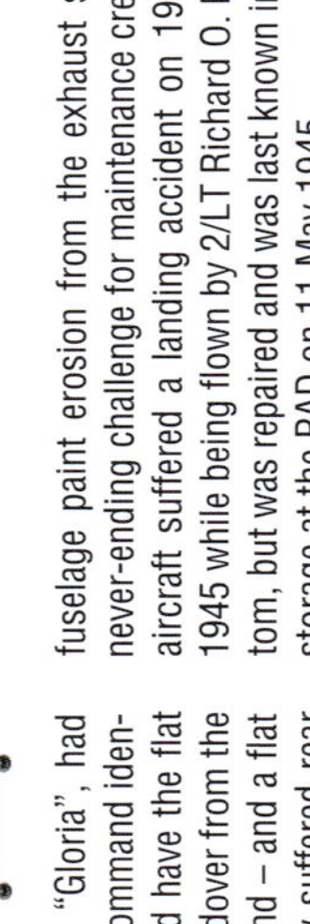

Bell P-39Q-5-BE Airacobra 42-20437, 32nd Fighter Squadron, Dakota Field, Aruba after 30 September 1943. Although initially assigned to Sixth Air Force on 13 August 1943, this and most other brand-new P-39Q-5s were moved on within a week to Aruba and the 32nd FS which by then was the sole fighter unit of the Antilles Air Command. It thus did not enjoy the attentions of the Panama Air Depot and operated in the open for more than nine months, probably accounting for the very worn appearance of her original, factory applied Olive Drab over Neutral Gray. However, at some point, the nose had been repainted and a very irregular demarcation was evident between the OD and the gray. Adorned with the yellow prop spinner (including nose cannon plug), fin cap and unit number 27, a small, brunette nude adorned the port side, reclining on a tropical beach, but without a specific name. Virtually all Sixth Air Force and AAC P-39Qs had their racks for the auxiliary fuel tank left in place permanently. This aircraft returned to the Canal Zone when the 32nd FS was reassigned to France Field in March 1944 and later served with the 24th Fighter Squadron (SE) before being scrapped on 16 June 1945.

Bell P-39Q-20-BE Airacobra 44-3093, 24th Fighter Squadron (SE), France Field, CZ, January 1944. The sixth P-39Q-20 to arrive in Panama, by this juncture the Sixth Air Force had abandoned the unique camouflage schemes of 1941-43 and fell into line with the world-wide USAAF standard factory-applied scheme of Olive Drab over a very regularly applied lower Neutral Gray. Unit number 18, "Gloria", had not yet had the unique XXVI Fighter Command identifier applied to her vertical fin but did have the flat white fin cap of that command – a holdover from the previous Panama Interceptor Command – and a flat white prop spinner. P-39s universally suffered rear fuselage paint erosion from the exhaust stacks, a never-ending challenge for maintenance crews. This aircraft suffered a landing accident on 19 January 1945 while being flown by 2/LT Richard O. Ransbottom, but was repaired and was last known in Class C storage at the PAD on 11 May 1945.

Bell P-39Q-10-BE Airacobra 42-20924, 24th Fighter Squadron (SE), France Field, CZ, after May 1944. The next-to-last P-39Q-10 to be assigned to Sixth Air Force, this aircraft arrived in the Command in early September 1943. It is unclear what unit she was assigned to prior to the 24th. She is unusual in having had splotches of darker (probably fresher) Olive Drab applied on her nose and rear fuselage – probably to address exhaust stains in the latter case – and stenciled unit number 44 in flat white on both her forward fuselage and drop tank. Her serial/radio call number was truncated to avoid the rudder hinge line and the XXVI Fighter Command identifier, "Triangle M" had been irregularly applied. The rudder trim tab and prop spinner were both, unusually, gloss white. This aircraft survived the war and was surveyed on 21 June 1945.

Bell P-39Q-20-BE Airacobra 44-3526, 24th Fighter Squadron (SE), France Field, CZ after March 1944. Although the 24th FS was later assigned the "Triangle M" identifier by XXVI Fighter Command (as noted in the upper drawing) when this aircraft arrived in early March 1944, the identifier was a "Circle M" instead. The reason for the change is unclear. Note that, for some reason, a black numeral 6 had at some point been painted under the yellow six of the serial/radio call sign on the rudder. What appears to be a unit insignia on the port door is in fact a personal insignia, similar to the pre-war unit insignia of the 88th Observation Squadron, with the legend "Gator Bait" in yellow arced over the top. This low-time aircraft was scrapped in July 1945.

Curtiss RP-40C-CU 41-13372, 30th Fighter Squadron, La Joya Auxiliary Aerodrome, Panama, 3 February 1944. A very well-traveled aircraft, this veteran had been assigned to the 36th Pursuit Group in Puerto Rico on 22 July 1941, but was transferred shortly after Peal Harbor to Panama to reinforce the defense. Later serving as far afield as Guatemala City, she suffered at least three known accidents before becoming a fighter-trainer with the 30th FS. Completely stripped of her earlier camouflage, with her rudder painted gray, she sported a red fin cap, a gloss black anti-glare panel and a small unit number 39 on the lower engine cowl. What appears to be a two-color prop spinner was actually different tones of metal. Incredibly, the aircraft was flown home to the Continental U.S. on 8 July 1944. The 30th FS was undoubtedly the largest squadron-sized unit in Sixth Air Force and was, essentially, the OTU for the command.

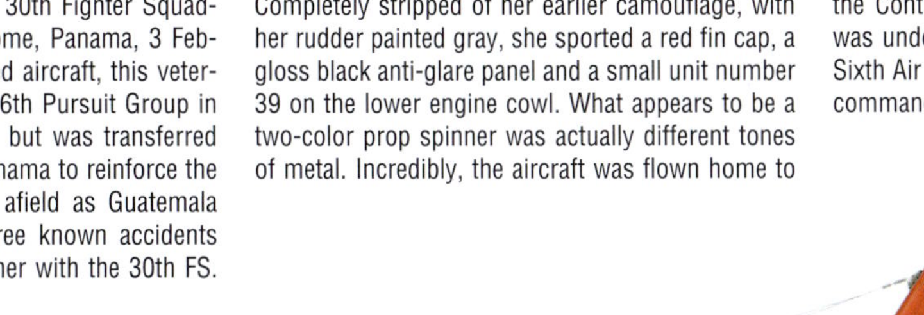

Curtiss P-40E-CU, 40-554, 30th Fighter Squadron, Chame Auxiliary Aerodrome, Panama, 21 December 1944. Yet another P-40 which was initially assigned to the 36th Pursuit Group in Puerto Rico in September 1941, 40-554, as of the date of this image, was a very high-time aircraft. Although assigned to the 30th FS, she still wore the XXVI Fighter Command identifier of the 24th FS (SE), with whom she had previously served, suggesting the accident of 21 December 1944 occurred shortly after reassignment. Remnants of her very irregular and extremely worn upper camouflage, the stenciled unit number 56 on the lower cowling, and the red and white prop spinner, were all holdovers from her lengthy assignment to the 24th FS. The aircraft was condemned after the accident at Chame.

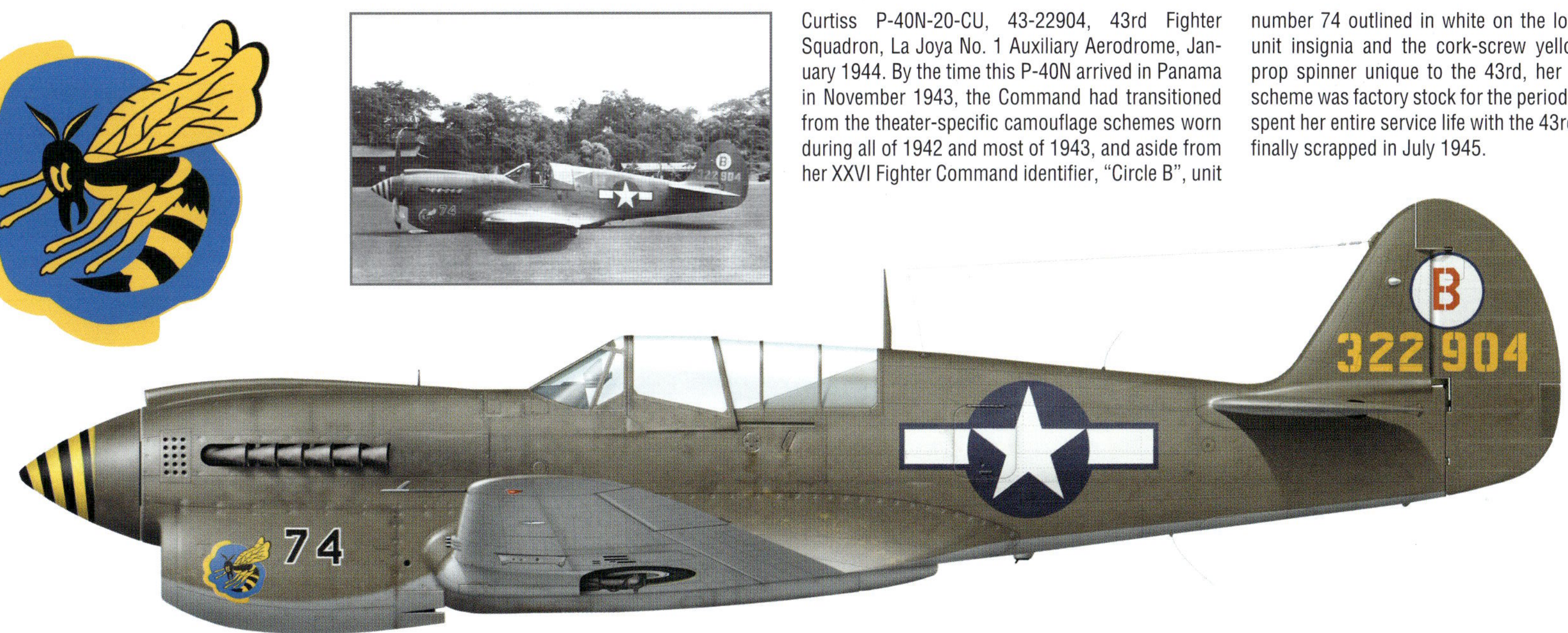

Curtiss P-40N-20-CU, 43-22904, 43rd Fighter Squadron, La Joya No. 1 Auxiliary Aerodrome, January 1944. By the time this P-40N arrived in Panama in November 1943, the Command had transitioned from the theater-specific camouflage schemes worn during all of 1942 and most of 1943, and aside from her XXVI Fighter Command identifier, "Circle B", unit number 74 outlined in white on the lower cowling, unit insignia and the cork-screw yellow-and-black prop spinner unique to the 43rd, her overall color scheme was factory stock for the period. This aircraft spent her entire service life with the 43rd FS and was finally scrapped in July 1945.

Curtiss P-40N-5-CU, 42-105299, Headquarters and Headquarters Squadron, XXVI Fighter Command, Albrook Field, CZ, December 1944. The third P-40N-5 to arrive in Panama, this aircraft wore factory-applied USAAF camouflage for the period, including the seldom noted random Dark Green splotches applied at various locations on the upper surfaces. The HHS, XXVI Fighter Command used the Command identifier "Lazy S" as shown, but also had a thin yellow band around the mid-fuselage – the only known instance of such an application in this unit, and probably signifying a leadership use. The aircraft survived the war, and was surplused in July 1945.

Curtiss P-36A, AC38-42, 24th Pursuit Squadron (I), 16th Pursuit Group, Albrook Field, Canal Zone, December 1939. When the used P-36As finally arrived in Panama to replace the Boeing P-26As, nearly all were initially assigned to the veteran 24th PS (I). Here, unit number 17 wears the distinctive leaping tiger squadron insignia, as well as the white forward engine cowling painted on all 16th PG (I) aircraft at the time, with a small black diamond on either side.

The anti-glare panel did not extend all the way over the nose. The aircraft was otherwise natural metal overall. The surviving P-36As were amongst the last Canal Zone based aircraft to be camouflaged late in 1941, as they were in such high demand for the rapidly expanding new units being formed that they could not be withdrawn from intensive training duties to be painted.

Curtiss P-36A, 10/32P, 52nd Pursuit Squadron, 32nd Pursuit Group, Rio Hato Auxiliary Aerodrome, Panama, late 1941. This Flight Leader's aircraft, denoted by the diagonal royal blue band outlined in thin white borders on the rear fuselage, presents something of an enigma. The 32nd PG was in the process of forming, and was seriously under-strength, so the number-within-unit (10) must be regarded with caution, as at this point the 52nd PS had but four aircraft on hand! The small number

36 on the natural metal portion of the cowling was probably left over from her previous assignment to the 24th PS (I), 16th PG and what appears to be a unit insignia on the mid-fuselage must have been a personal mark of the pilot or Flight Leader. It appears to be similar to that of the 65th PS, which did not serve in Panama, but may have had some personal significance to the pilot.

Curtiss P-36A, AC38-60, 33/16P, 29th Pursuit Squadron (I), 16th Pursuit Group (I), Rio Hato Auxiliary Aerodrome, late 1941. This aircraft had arrived in Panama in August 1939 from Selfridge Field, MI, and is seen here in the markings of the Squadron Commander of the 29th PS (I), signified by the two red bands, edged in white, on the rear fuselage, and the unit insignia on the mid-fuselage. Note that, in accordance with Air Corps regulations at the time, the aircraft is very nearly marked properly, including a repeat of the individual identifier, 16P33, under the leading edge of each wing. The segmented, red/white wheel disc covers were, unusually, painted on nearly all Sixth Air Force/Caribbean Air Force P-36As – not as a unit marking, although the 29th PS was credited with pioneering this marking, but to provide visual evidence to the observers in the control tower that the wheels were in fact down when the aircraft was approaching to land. The first retractable gear fighter aircraft type to be assigned to the CAC, the P-36As, suffered an inordinate number of wheels-up landings by pilots who had previously flown only fixed gear P-26As. This aircraft was transferred to Brazil in March 1942 under Lend-Lease.

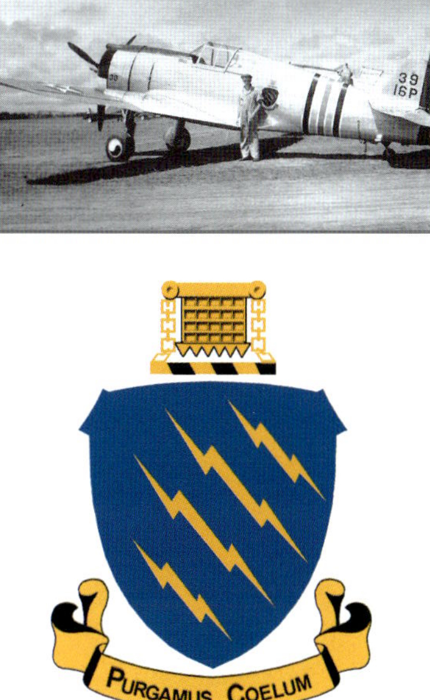

Curtiss P-36A, 39/16P, Headquarters and Headquarters Squadron, 16th Pursuit Group (I), Rio Hato Auxiliary Aerodrome, Panama, late 1941. The Group Commanders aircraft, bearing the colors of the three subordinate squadrons on the rear fuselage and segmented nose cowling, had apparently previously been assigned to the 29th PS (I), as the individual number is very high – most aircraft assigned to a Group Headquarters being very low, single-digit numbers. It also bears the red/white wheel covers usually associated with the 29th PS, but in fact applied to nearly all P-36As assigned to Panama. The identifier, 16P39, is repeated under the leading edge of the wing, and probably in much larger characters on the inboard upper wing panels as well.

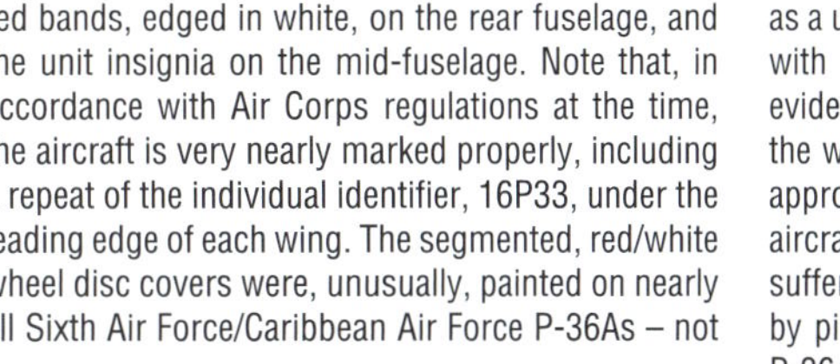

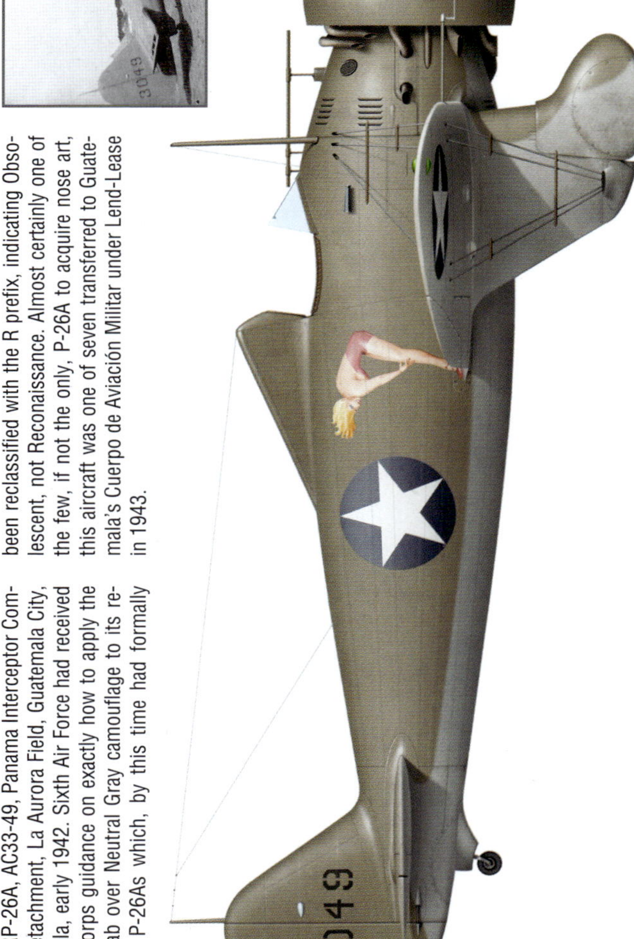

Boeing RP-26A, AC33-49, Panama Interceptor Command Detachment, La Aurora Field, Guatemala City, Guatemala, early 1942. Sixth Air Force had received no Air Corps guidance on exactly how to apply the Olive Drab over Neutral Gray camouflage to its remaining P-26As which, by this time had formally been reclassified with the R prefix, indicating Obsolescent, not Reconaissance. Almost certainly one of the few, if not the only, P-26A to acquire nose art, this aircraft was one of seven transferred to Guatemala's Cuerpo de Aviación Militar under Lend-Lease in 1943.

Boeing "PT-26A", number 43 (USAAC AC33-123), Cuerpo de Aviación Militar, Guatemala, 1943. As soon at Guatemala received its seven P-26As which, for administrative reasons, the U.S. Munitions Assignment Board (Air) invariably cited as type PT-26A to cloak the fact that fighters were being provided to a Central American air arm, the service painted them with French green overall, except for the engine cowlings which, for some reason, were left in their former USAAF Olive Drab. Number 43 and most of the others also initially wore a caricature of a legendary indigenous warrior on the mid-fuselage side as shown, consisting of a red outline, white field, flesh-colored features and silver battle dress. Later, the Guatemalan "PT-26As" were remarked and wore a variety of spectacular color schemes and special markings, two surviving to return to the U.S. – the sole, genuine remaining examples, one at National Museum of the USAF and the other at Planes of Fame.